From Pigeons to People

Also by
ELIZABETH HALL

Phoebe Snow
Stand up, Lucy
Why We Do What We Do

Elizabeth Hall

FROM PIGEONS TO PEOPLE

A Look at Behavior Shaping

1975
HOUGHTON MIFFLIN COMPANY BOSTON

Acknowledgement

All my thanks to Paul Chance, Ph.D.,
and Scott O'Dell.
The first made sure the text was accurate;
the second kept me from wandering
into thickets of jargon.

156.385
H141

Library of Congress Cataloging in Publication Data

Hall, Elizabeth, 1929–
  From pigeons to people.

  SUMMARY: A discussion of modern psychology with
emphasis on the terms, methods, and theories of be-
havior-shaping.
  1. Operant conditioning — Juvenile literature.
[1. Operant conditioning. 2. Conditioned response.
3. Psychology] I. Title.
BF319.5.06H34   156'.3'85   75-17030
ISBN 0-395-21894-2

For Lauren Elizabeth Di Prima

CONTENTS

From Pigeons to People

1

Pigeons, Pills and the Pelican

One day, almost twenty years ago, a young psychologist made a tour of a drug factory.

Among other things, he noticed that seventy women spent their entire day watching empty drug capsules roll past them on a moving belt. Whenever one of these workers saw a capsule that was dented, bumpy or the wrong color, she picked it up and threw it away.

Thom Verhave, the young psychologist, could see that this was a boring job. He wondered if pigeons could learn to spot bad capsules, called skags, as well as the women did.

He went back to his laboratory and set to work.

Thom Verhave made a machine that sent two capsules rolling past one pigeon every second. The pigeon's job was to peer through a small window and then peck three times on the window whenever a light shone on a capsule.

If the capsule was good, the bird pecked on a key that turned off the light and moved the next capsule up for inspection. If the capsule was bad, the pigeon pecked twice more on the little window and the skag was rejected.

Within a week, two of his pigeons had learned their job and were pecking away in his lab. The birds had learned to detect the skags just as fast as the women did. And what was more, they didn't get bored.

Some years before, another psychologist, B. F. Skinner, decided that pigeons were smart enough to direct missiles to their targets.

His work began in the spring of 1940 at the University of Minnesota. War was raging in Europe, but the United States had not yet entered the conflict. Skinner wanted to find some defense against the German bombers that were dropping explosives on cities filled with civilians.

In his first system, the pigeon was put into a jacket and harnessed inside a missile. The movement of the bird's head, as it stretched to eat grain from the center of a bull's eye, would direct the missile up, down or from side to side. But the United States had no ground-to-air missiles, and the Air Force therefore showed no interest in the project.

Several years later, with the United States in the war, both business and the government suddenly became interested in Skinner's pigeons.

They began to test a missile, which they called the Pelican — a glider steered by wings — in a secret place in New Jersey. The trouble was they couldn't figure out a way to steer the thing.

Working with other psychologists, Skinner began again and developed a more complicated but accurate system.

A lens in the nose of the missile threw a picture of the bomb's target onto a screen that the pigeon could easily reach. By pecking at the picture of the target — the ship, plane or building that the bomb was to hit — the bird caused air valves that controlled the bomb's path to pop open.

In one of the early demonstrations of the new peck-guided system, a bird kept a dummy missile on its course — headed straight for the spot where two city streets crossed — for five minutes. If the pigeon had stopped pecking for even a second, the bomb would have missed its target.

To make sure that a single pigeon did not grow tired or bored, like the women in the factory, and choose the wrong target, Skinner and his team harnessed three pigeons into the nose of a Pelican missile. Each pigeon had its own screen. At least two of them had to agree on the exact target before the bomb would go hurtling toward it. The birds learned to navigate, to the surprise of the scientists, "better than radar."

Pigeons are not highly intelligent.

A pigeon does not reject a skag because it knows that a defective capsule will not hold the right drug dosage. It can't learn the multiplication tables, let alone trigonometry or celestial navigation. It has no idea that its metal cage is part of a bomb meant to destroy cities and human beings — as well as itself.

Yet there is nothing mysterious about these accomplishments. Both Verhave and Skinner taught their pigeons complicated tasks by giving them grain when the birds behaved as they were supposed to. This method of rewarding an animal after it does what you want it to do is called *positive reinforcement.* And positive reinforcement is the backbone of *behavior shaping.*

Behavior shaping is also called *behavior modification,* which means a change in behavior. Sometimes it is shortened to *behavior mod,* or even *bemod.* And with a distinct lack of respect, behavior shapers have even been called the bemod squad. Whatever term is used, the meaning is the same.

These techniques, first developed by Skinner, have for many years been used to train animals. Whenever you see an animal perform in the movies, the circus or on television, you can be fairly sure that its tricks are based on Skinner's techniques.

But his research has moved out of experimental laboratories and beyond the world of animal shows.

The same principles that taught pigeons to peck for skags are now used in prisons, mental hospitals, nursing homes, factories, day-care centers, classrooms and in the home. Because they are so successful in changing what we do, more and more doctors, teachers, wardens, businessmen and parents are turning to Skinner's methods.

For many years, when only animals, prisoners and mental patients were the subjects, behavior modifiers worked quietly to change the behavior of their charges. But now that behavior shaping has reached into the lives of us all, a public argument has begun to rage over the methods and the ideas behind them.

The argument has always been in the background, in one form or another. Although Verhave's pigeons were at least as efficient as the women on the pill inspection line, the big drug company that paid for the research never hired pigeon pill inspectors. And while Skinner's pigeons were "better than radar," Project Pigeon never got off the ground.

Many people in the midst of the argument don't bother to find out how behavior shaping works or what ideas lie behind it. Loud voices on one side promise that behavior shaping will lead us into a peaceful, happy world. Others, just as loud, warn that it lures us into a brave new world of dictators.

A closer look at this controversial field may help

separate the hopes and the threats from the real programs that now go on across the country. With the facts before us, we will be in a better position to judge both the warnings and the promises.

2

The Birth of Behaviorism

Behaviorists developed the methods that people use to change the behavior of animals or other persons. Most behaviorists trace their ideas to the work of B. F. Skinner. But behaviorism didn't start with Skinner.

It all began in Russia in 1905 in the laboratories of Ivan Pavlov, who was not a psychologist but a physiologist.

Behaviorists and other psychologists study what human beings and animals do, hoping that their experiments will turn up rules that can predict what people will do in the future and why they will do it.

Physiologists study what goes on inside. How the heart pumps blood. How the blood carries nourishment to all parts of the body. How the brain works. How the glands make substances that turn a child into a man or woman.

Pavlov was studying the way a digestive system breaks down food into the sugars, vitamins, minerals and proteins that nourish the body, when he happened upon his discovery. Dogs were his subjects.

Pavlov noted that the instant a spoonful of meat powder was placed in a dog's mouth, the dog began to drool. Saliva began to flow and thus the digestive process started. The food was an *unconditioned stimulus*. When the dog tasted it, he naturally responded by drooling.

Before long, however, his dogs began to drool before the powder was placed in their mouths. Just the sight of the man who fed them made saliva flow.

Pavlov set up an experiment to see if he could make a dog drool whenever he wished it to. He used a tuning fork, a small device that always produces the same note when struck. In each test he struck the tuning fork, then put the meat powder in the dog's mouth.

When he began the experiment, the dog's mouth stayed dry until it had tasted the powder. But after a few tries, the dog began to drool the moment it heard the sound of the tuning fork. Pavlov had *conditioned* the dog to respond to the sound just as the other dogs had learned to respond to the sight of the man who fed them.

The sound had become a *conditioned stimulus.* It caused the dogs to act as if they were being fed.

But the dogs had no control over their responses to either the sight of their keeper or to the sound of the tuning fork. They learned to drool without knowing what they were doing, just as your own mouth might water at the sight of a juicy steak.

Psychologists who went no further than Pavlov's *classical conditioning* could never shape the complicated behavior produced by Skinner's followers. Although classical conditioning is a powerful tool, its use is too obvious to have caused the storm of controversy that now swirls around behaviorists.

About the same time that Pavlov was working in Russia, an American psychologist, John B. Watson, invented the term *behaviorism* and called himself a *behaviorist.* Watson didn't care what went on inside people. He was not interested in what people thought or felt, only in what they did.

Like Pavlov he believed that classical conditioning was the basis of learning. In the same way that Pavlov taught dogs to drool whenever they heard a tuning fork, Watson taught a baby to cry whenever he saw anything white and fuzzy.

He brought Albert, who was nine months old, into his laboratory and showed him a tame white rat. Albert did not cry and even tried to play with this new toy.

Once Watson decided that Albert was not afraid of the rat, he was ready to begin. Each time he showed Albert the rat, someone made a loud noise just behind the baby's head. Soon, each time Albert saw the rat, he cried. And he cried whenever he saw a white rabbit, a fur scarf or a man with a white beard. He had been conditioned to fear white, fuzzy objects.

About 1930, the same B. F. Skinner who taught pigeons to steer bombs was a student at Harvard University. The work of Pavlov and Watson inspired him to experiment with animals in his own laboratory. Skinner chose rats. In the basement of the biology building he began to condition the small animals to press bars if they wanted food.

But Skinner was not using classical conditioning. His rats were not responding to a sound that buzzed or a light that flashed each time food dropped into their cups.

They were working for their dinner. Instead of responding to a stimulus, they were responding without one. They pressed the bar to make food appear because in the past food had appeared when they pressed the bar.

This was a new kind of conditioning, and Skinner called it *operant conditioning*. The animal had to do something to earn its reward. It had to operate on the world around it.

Operant conditioning is the method that behavior shapers are using today in prisons, hospitals, schools and businesses to change the behavior of convicts, patients, students and workers.

Skinner's rats learned through positive reinforcement.

Each time a rat did what Skinner wanted it to do, a pellet of food dropped into its cup. In the beginning all he wanted the rat to do was to press the bar. The food reinforced bar-pressing. It made it more likely that the rat would press the bar again.

Before Skinner could study the rat's responses to its conditioning, he had to be able to control the rat's world. All the sights, sounds, smells, tastes, objects, animals and people that make up a world are called the *environment*.

Skinner controlled the rat's environment by building a small soundproofed box that held only a cup for food and a lever. The box had solid sides so that the rat could not see what went on in the laboratory, but it was ventilated for the rat's comfort. Any change in the animal's behavior, Skinner had decided, must come from the experiment.

For several days the rat earned a pellet of food each time it pressed the lever. Then for a day or two no food dropped into the cup, no matter how often the rat pressed. When food failed to appear, the rat always gave up and stopped pressing the lever.

Skinner called this *extinction*. The rat's bar-pressing response had become as extinct as the dodo.

One Saturday afternoon Skinner looked in his box of food pellets and discovered that he would run out of rat rewards before he could get a new supply. He thought of a new idea.

Instead of giving the rat a pellet each time it pressed the lever, he set the food dispenser on the box so that only one pellet a minute dropped into the cup. No matter how often the rat pressed, no matter how hard, only one of its responses was rewarded each minute.

To Skinner's surprise the rat kept pressing, pressing often enough to get a pellet every minute.

He next tried another system of rewards. Each rat had to press the lever twenty times to get a single pellet. But the animals soon learned the new schedule. They made twenty presses often enough to keep their stomachs comfortably full.

Skinner had stumbled onto another principle of operant conditioning, the principle of *intermittent reinforcement*. He had found that a response does not have to be rewarded each time it is made, just often enough to keep the animal hoping that a pellet will drop into the cup the next time it presses the lever.

Intermittent reinforcement turned out to be more powerful than constant reinforcement.

One pigeon in Skinner's laboratory learned that grain sometimes appeared after it pecked a key. When the grain stopped coming altogether, the pigeon pecked the key 10,000 times before it stopped. That bird was like the gamblers in Las Vegas who will play a slot machine for hours. They know the machine will reward them only after they have pulled the lever many times. But they keep on pulling, hoping that the next time they will hit the jackpot. Slot machines pay off on a schedule of intermittent reinforcement.

After Skinner had worked with his rats for a number of years, he wrote a book, *The Behavior of Organisms.* He described all of his experiments and everything he had found out about operant conditioning. In the book he said that he had discovered more than how to make rats press levers. He believed that he had discovered how all animals and people learn.

His book appeared in 1938, but did not have much impact. A number of psychologists began to do the same kinds of animal experiments, but while they learned a lot about rats and pigeons and dogs, psychologists who worked with people showed little interest.

The psychologists who ignored the experiments should have paid attention, because the ones who did were finding out a lot about why animals do what they do. Among the things the new behaviorists found out was that giving rewards, or positive reinforcement, wasn't the only way to change behavior. You could also make an animal so uncomfortable that he would do whatever you wanted.

Training an animal in this way is called *escape training,* because the animal learns in order to escape pain or discomfort. The pain acts as *negative reinforcement,* because escaping the discomfort rewards the animal. It is likely to repeat whatever action stopped the pain.

Psychologists often used electric shock in escape training.

O. Hobart Mowrer made a small box with a floor of metal grids. The grids were wired so that electric current ran through the floor *except* when a small lever at one end of the cage was pressed. Mowrer put a rat in the box and turned on the electricity. Naturally, the rat found it extremely unpleasant and tried to flee.

It ran across the box and inadvertently pressed the lever. The electric shock stopped. When it took its paw off the lever, the shock began once more. The rat, however, learned fast. By the tenth time Mowrer dropped it into the box, the rat pressed the lever the second the shock began — and kept pressing it.

Negative reinforcement works with people, too. You learn to get yourself out of uncomfortable situations by repeating responses that have rescued you in the past. Each time you reach for an aspirin when you have a headache, you are responding to negative reinforcement. In the past, taking aspirin has been followed by the disappearance of your headache. You may find it hard to connect lever-pressing to escape electric shock with taking aspirin to escape an aching head, but behaviorists believe that the same kind of learning goes on in both cases.

Nearly everybody who heard about negative reinforcement in the laboratory said that the psychologists were punishing the rats, and punishment was old stuff. Human beings had been using punishment for years with animals and people, too. Sometimes it worked and sometimes it didn't.

They were wrong, because negative reinforcement is very different from *punishment.*

Punishment and negative reinforcement can be the same stimulus. A shock is a shock is a shock. But in punishment the animal *gets* the shock after it responds in a certain way, whereas in negative reinforcement, the shock *stops* after the animal responds in that way.

Punishment can change behavior, but punishment comes *after* a person or animal has done something. The discomfort or pain of punishment is supposed to teach a rat never to repeat what it did before it was punished.

Negative reinforcement makes an animal act. Punishment stops it from acting. As years of human history have shown, punishment doesn't always work.

When psychologists tried punishing rats for pushing levers, the rats stopped pushing the levers. But when food came along with the electric shock, the rats stopped pushing the lever only as long as each push gave them a shock. As soon as the electricity was turned off, the rats began pressing the lever just as often as they did before.

The positive reinforcement of the food was stronger than the punishment the rats had learned might come along with their reward. They took a chance, like the gambler who risks "one more" quarter in the slot machine.

Experiments with animals taught psychologists that positive reinforcement was the most effective way to change behavior. An animal often learned more slowly with positive reinforcement than with punishment, but once its behavior changed, the change lasted longer. And positive reinforcement was both pleasanter to give and to get than either negative reinforcement or punishment.

All three methods worked. With positive reinforcement, negative reinforcement and punishment at their command, psychologists had the tools they needed to change human behavior.

3

Strictly Animals

Psychologists now had the tools to change human behavior, but most of them kept on working with animals in psychology laboratories.

In colleges across the country, white rats ran down narrow corridors, learning to take the turns that would bring them to food. Other rats learned to press bars and pigeons dutifully pecked at keys.

These experiments taught psychologists a lot about rats and pigeons. They discovered, for example, that pigeons can tell the difference between a red light and an orange light, and that a rat can learn to lift more than twice its own weight.

The weight-lifting rat, appropriately named Hercules, lived in a cage in a college laboratory. When the experiment began, Hercules was just an ordinary white male rat with pink eyes and a long tail. If Hercules had any special talent, the psychologists didn't notice it.

Each time he went near the food cup in his cage, Hercules heard a loud click, a light went on near the cup, and a pellet of food appeared. Once Hercules connected the click and the light with food, the experimenter was ready to begin.

Now the click, the light and the food appeared only when Hercules moved toward a bar that was next to the food cup. Then only when Hercules touched the bar. Soon Hercules had to press the bar down before he was reinforced. By a series of small steps, the experimenters were shaping the rat's behavior.

His weight-lifting lessons then began. Gradually, the experimenter added small weights to the other end of the bar. When Hercules pressed down the bar to get food, he had to use enough strength to lift the added weight. In just a few hours, Hercules — who weighed only 250 grams — had learned to push away until he lifted 515 grams of metal weights.

Other rats have learned equally spectacular feats by the same method.

Barnabus, another male rat, learned to scramble up a circular staircase, cross a moat, climb a ladder, pedal a small red car, run up a second set of stairs, squeeze through a glass tube and ride down a tiny elevator to get his food. As in the case of Hercules, psychologists taught Barnabus his two-minute one-rat show a single step at a time, until a series of tiny acts formed a lengthy chain of complicated behavior.

The secret in teaching such dazzling chains of behavior is always to begin with the last step and work backward. Each time the animal masters a link in the chain, it must learn one more link before it gets its reward.

Pigeons, the other favorite laboratory animal, learned their share of fancy tricks. B. F. Skinner, who ingeniously taught pigeons to guide bombs, also trained the birds in pleasanter tasks. Under his guidance, pigeons learned to peck out simple tunes on a xylophone, to bowl in their own miniature alley and to play a fast game of Ping-Pong. The famous Ping-Pong players were reinforced each time they pecked the ball hard enough to send it flying past their opponent.

Psychologists found that the tools of conditioning worked well with all animals. Keller and Marian Breland, a pair of psychologists in Arkansas, had such success in shaping animal behavior that they opened a business of training animal performers. The Brelands dressed hens in costumes, put shoes on their claws and taught them to tap-dance.

One of their star performers was "Priscilla, the Fastidious Pig." Attractive and well-groomed Priscilla toured the country, advertising General Mills products at conventions and fairs. During her act, Priscilla pretended to be a housewife. She turned on a radio, ate breakfast at a table, picked up dirty clothes and stowed them neatly in a hamper, then vacuumed the floor with a toy vacuum cleaner.

Her housework done, Priscilla picked out her favorite food from among several dishes of commercial livestock feed. Thanks to her careful training, Priscilla always chose the product from General Mills. To wind up her performance, Priscilla answered questions from the audience, making lights flash "Yes" or "No" in response to the queries.

Priscilla was not a special pig. Because pigs grow fast, and large pigs are hard to ship from one city to another, about every four months a new pig became the star of the pig world. It appeared that any pig could learn to become an actor.

But behavior shapers have gone beyond fun and games.

In Ohio three psychologists have used conditioning to make the lives of pet owners happy. David Tuber, David Hothersall and Victoria Voith tackle pets with behavior problems such as biting, chewing the furniture or misusing the family carpet as a toilet.

One of their clients was an English sheep dog named Higgins that was scared to death of thunderstorms. As soon as the big dog heard the roll of thunder, he began to pace about the room, to drool and to pant.

When the storm began in earnest, Higgins would hurl himself against walls, doors, windows and people in an attempt to get away. Once a thunderstorm began when his owner was sitting with Higgins inside a small sportscar. Since Higgins weighed over one hundred pounds, his sudden explosion as the car traveled down the highway turned his fear from an annoyance into a danger. Although his owner pulled the car safely off the road, she decided that Higgins must either overcome his fear or find another home.

When presented with the problem, the psychologists at Ohio State University decided to condition the dog to endure thunderstorms.

They first got Higgins to lie down while a recording of extremely faint thunder played softly in the background. Then, each time they worked with the dog, the volume was slowly increased. They also gave Higgins a chocolate bar each time the thunder began to roll. Before long Higgins was able to control himself.

He never learned to enjoy the crack of lightning and the roll of thunder — who does? But Higgins lived happily ever after. The big dog had come to associate a storm with chocolate candy, just as Pavlov's dogs associated the sound of a tuning fork with food, and little Albert associated white, furry animals with a fearful noise.

Higgins was cured by classical conditioning. His candy bar did not depend on any of his actions. It came no matter what he did.

In Skinner's operant conditioning, on the other hand, the animal must behave as the experimenter wishes before it gets its reward. The psychologists who helped Higgins used Skinner's operant conditioning with other problem animals, like the terrier named Sandy who liked to bite his three-year-old mistress.

Whenever Jenny and Sandy played together, Sandy would nip the little girl. What's more, he began to nip all children. When Tuber and his colleagues watched the pair romping together, they discovered that the play was so rough that Sandy's use of his teeth was not surprising, but natural.

Punishing Sandy with slaps or exile was no solution to the problem. It was plain that both the dog and the girl were equally responsible for the nips.

The psychologists decided that the parents should train Sandy and Jenny separately. Jenny learned to pet a stuffed toy. Whenever she petted it gently, her mother rewarded her with a piece of candy. At the same time, Sandy was taught to be patient. When he obeyed his master and sat quietly, he earned a slice of hot dog.

At last the moment came to bring the playmates together. Sandy was told to sit. Her mother then asked Jenny to pet Sandy gently, but just once, as she had petted the stuffed animal. Sandy got his hot dog and Jenny got her candy.

At the next stage, Jenny was asked to pet the dog in two places to earn her candy and Sandy had to tolerate two pets before he was fed. Each time the two were brought together, it took more petting and more patience for Jenny and Sandy to earn the rewards.

The conditioning succeeded. Sandy never nips Jenny, but Jenny's parents see that the dog and child play the petting game once in a while just to make sure that the two don't forget what they have learned. And whenever new children are introduced to Sandy, they, too, are asked to play the successful petting game.

It seemed as if psychologists now could do anything. Give them an animal, tell them what you want, and within a few days or weeks or months at the most they would cure faults or produce an actor that appeared so human that even scientists would "ooh" and "aah" at its feats.

The Brelands were the most successful behavior changers. They trained more than 6000 animals of thirty-eight different kinds, including reindeer, cows, crows and even whales.

But it was the Brelands who first reported that behavior shaping did not always work.

One of their failures was a raccoon. The trick seemed simple. All the raccoon had to do was to pick up coins and deposit them in a piggy bank. Raccoons had learned much harder tricks. Besides, this raccoon was quite tame.

The conditioning started smoothly.

The raccoon quickly learned to pick up a single coin to get food. As the training progressed, he had to place the coin in the bank before he received a reward. The raccoon found it hard to let go of the coin. He would start to put the coin into the slot, then he'd rub it against the bank, pull it out and clutch at it tightly. Not for several seconds would he give up the coin, dropping it slowly into the slot.

Now the Brelands decided that he must deposit two coins before he was reinforced. But like a miser, he held on to the coins. He rubbed them together. He dipped them into the bank, only to pull them back at the last minute.

The Brelands stopped rewarding him. His behavior got worse. The experiment was a total failure.

That failure, however, was only one of many. There were other animals — hamsters, whales, cats, rabbits, cows, pigs and chickens — that seemed unable to learn some of the seemingly simple tricks that the Brelands tried to teach them.

Behavior shaping *didn't* always work. It didn't work, they found, when an animal's instinctive behavior interfered with the goals of the experimenter.

Instinctive behavior is behavior that an animal performs without teaching, although sometimes the animal must practice. It appears, as if by magic, when an animal meets a situation that calls for that behavior. Chickens peck, pigs root, birds fly, human beings walk. And raccoons wash their food before they eat it.

Although the Brelands' raccoon didn't intend to eat the coins, when he rubbed them together, he was showing what psychologists call "washing behavior." As raccoons rub their food and dip it in water, they not only wash dirt from their dinner, they also remove the shells of shrimp or crayfish.

In asking the raccoon to deposit coins in a piggy bank, the Brelands were trying to make the little animal resist millions of years of raccoon behavior. And the raccoon just couldn't do it, even though he knew that dropping coins in a bank would bring him food.

He was, in short, not a piece of putty. He behaved in certain ways that he had inherited along with the shape of his small hands and furry coat — and he would keep behaving in those ways no matter how hard psychologists worked to change them.

Now psychologists know that there are limits to the powers of reinforcement. They know that when they do not interfere with inherited behavior, dazzling performances result. And they know that when they use their techniques on animals more intelligent than rats or raccoons or pigs, the results are spectacular — and also have serious implications.

4

Almost Human

As surprising as the feats of Priscilla Pig and Hercules Rat may seem, each animal merely learned to produce whatever behavior the trainers decided to shape.

In Hawaii, however, dolphins, which are highly intelligent animals, learned to be creative. They didn't paint, play the piano or write poetry, but they learned to invent new kinds of behavior — to the amazement of psychologists.

The case of the creative dolphins took place at Sea Life Park in Hawaii, where each day dolphins per-

form for thousands of tourists. It began with Karen
Pryor and a dolphin named Malia.

Karen Pryor wanted to show the tourists how dolphins were educated at Sea Life Park, so she instructed the trainer to give Malia bits of fish when
she acted in a new way, a way that was not already a
part of the show. The trainer waited until Malia invented a new kind of behavior, then fed her. If by
chance the new behavior was a tail slap, he reinforced her each time she slapped her tail against the
water. Soon Malia was slapping her tail over and
over again.

At the next performance the trainer didn't reward
Malia for a tail slap. If he was to show the audience
how dolphins were trained at Sea Life Park, he
needed to reinforce a new behavior.

He watched Malia and waited, ignoring the slap of
her tail. Malia gave up. It seemed as if she were
disgusted with her trainer. Then suddenly she
began to spin in the water. The trainer promptly
reinforced the spin and fed her each time she completed the new antic.

Sea Life Park gives five shows a day. Before many
days had passed, Malia and her trainer had exhausted
all the normal things that dolphins do. It appeared
as if the Park would either have to give up the training demonstration or else find a different dolphin.

Then, to everyone's surprise, Malia began to produce new tricks. She behaved in ways that none of
the trainers had ever seen before. She had learned

that her trainer wanted new acts, so she thoughtfully created them!

The staff at Sea Life Park was astounded. They wondered if Malia was a brilliant dolphin — an Einstein among dolphins — or if other dolphins could learn to create new acts. So they chose Hou, a dolphin that had always seemed timid and rarely did things on her own.

Before long, timid Hou was just as creative as Malia. Once she produced an aerial flip that took her out of the water and ended with her skidding on the floor of the tank. Another time she stood on her tail and clapped her jaws at her trainer, showering him with water.

Pryor and the other trainers finally had to stop the experiment. But they didn't stop because Hou ran out of ideas. No, the experiment in creativity stopped because Hou's tricks became too complicated. The trainers had to keep track of all her tricks so that more than one trainer could work with her. But now the dolphin was inventing such intricate antics that they couldn't record them.

Once the school for creativity ended, the trainers expected Malia and Hou to go back to behaving like other dolphins. Malia and Hou did play their parts in the show, but the training in creativity left its mark.

Hou began to leap over the tank partitions to visit other dolphins. And one day when the trainer was busy at another tank, Malia jumped from the water, slid across the cement floor and tapped him on the ankle with her snout.

It seems that if an animal is regularly reinforced for being creative, it will continue to be creative at other times and in other places.

The dolphins of Sea Life Park showed that reinforcement was a more powerful tool than the behavior shapers had claimed. Used properly it could produce behavior that behaviorists had never dreamed of.

The next success came when patient psychologists succeeded in breaking the barrier that most wise men said could never be broken. They taught chimpanzees to "talk."

The chimp throat is not flexible enough to shape the sounds of human speech, but chimps can communicate. Some have learned to use their hands to form the sign language of deaf people. Others talk by placing little pieces of colored plastic on a board, each piece standing for a different word.

At the Yerkes Primate Center in Georgia, a chimp named Lana can read and write. Lana doesn't pick up a pen and scrawl words on paper. Instead, she uses a special typewriter that is hooked up to a computer.

What's more, she doesn't type English, but a special language called Yerkish, a language more like Egyptian hieroglyphics than like English. Lana lives in a special room, and she can have anything she wants. But in order to get it, she must type her request into the computer.

When Lana wants a banana, she pulls down a bar that turns on the computer and begins to push the keys.

On each of the fifty plastic keys is a Yerkish symbol that stands for a particular word. As Lana pushes a key, the symbol she has pressed shows up on a screen above the keyboard. To get her banana, Lana must push seven keys in the proper order: PLEASE/MACHINE/GIVE/PIECE/OF/BANANA/PERIOD. The period key tells the computer that the sentence is finished.

If Lana wants to look at the outside world, she types: PLEASE/MACHINE/MAKE/WINDOW/OPEN/PE-RIOD. The computer then opens a window in the side of her concrete room. If she wants to play with her trainer, she types: PLEASE/TIM/COME/INTO/ROOM/PERIOD.

Lana can make the computer show her movies; play music; or deliver water, juice, apples or M&M's. She can ask Tim to tickle her. When Lana operates her Yerkish typewriter, she moves so fast that her fingers blur across the keys.

Lana can *read* Yerkish, too.

Duane Rumbaugh, the psychologist in charge of Lana, found that she had learned to read. He already knew that she recognized the Yerkish symbols, because he kept changing the position of the symbols on the keyboard so that she could not learn that, for example, apple was the third key from the right on the second row.

To check Lana's reading ability, Rumbaugh devised a completion test. Using controls outside Lana's room, Rumbaugh typed the beginning of a sentence, then stopped. Lana watched as the symbols lit up on the keyboard. If the sentence was correct, she would finish it. If the sentence was incorrect, Lana would press the period key, clearing the computer for another request.

Rumbaugh taught Lana to read and write using positive reinforcement.

At first the chimp had to press only one key: BANANA or JUICE or M & M to get her reward. Gradually Rumbaugh shaped her behavior, making her press longer and longer strings of keys before the machine paid off.

But Lana learned to clear the computer by herself. As she began to use more and more keys, sometimes she made a mistake. She might type words in the wrong order, such as PLEASE/WINDOW/MAKE/MACHINE/OPEN/PERIOD. Or she might make a request that was not part of the rules, such as PLEASE/MACHINE/COME/INTO/ROOM/PERIOD. When she pushed the period to signal that this kind of sentence was complete, the machine just wiped out all the symbols on the screen and waited for her to start over.

Before long Lana discovered that whenever she made a mistake there was no point in going further.

Now when she presses the wrong key, she immediately pushes the period and begins again.

Lana knows fifty words, but chimps who use sign language or pieces of plastic know one hundred and fifty.

Washoe, who moves her hands rapidly through the signs of the deaf, and Sarah, who places chips of brightly colored plastic on a board, combine and recombine their words to say many more things than Lana can manage. The 150 words of Sarah and Washoe fall far short of the 1200-word vocabulary possessed by the typical child of less than four. But the techniques of the behavior shaper managed to turn dumb beasts into animals that can converse with people and with other animals about many things.

Even before Lana and Washoe and Sarah began to talk, and before Hou and Malia learned to create new behavior, other psychologists turned from reinforcing animals to reinforcing human beings.

5

People in a Box

Psychologists believed that the same techniques they had used on rats and pigeons would also work on people, but they needed to prove it.

The task seemed difficult, because people can't be kept in cages. They can go anywhere they please, which meant that psychologists could not prove that their manipulations had caused the changes in their subjects' behavior.

Skinner controlled the world of his rats by shutting them away from all the sights and sounds that might interfere with his experiments. Psychologists needed to find the same sort of world, a place where they could control the lives of their subjects in the same way.

Patients in mental hospitals were already shut away from life's distractions. What's more, they had little to say about their fates. Their lives were ruled by hospital regulations. This made it simple to control their worlds. Mental hospitals were a perfect place for psychologists to try out their new techniques.

Many in these hospitals are intelligent human beings whose behavior has become bizarre or who cannot handle the details of daily life. Others were born so severely retarded that they don't even know that details exist.

By 1949 one psychologist had been able to change the behavior of what doctors called a "vegetative idiot." Paul Fuller worked with an eighteen-year-old boy who had never learned to speak or to respond to others. Day after day he sat in one place like a vegetable and even had to be fed by others.

Fuller shaped the boy's behavior, just as the Brelands had shaped the behavior of Priscilla Pig. At first he gave the boy a drink of warm, sweet milk each time he moved his arm, then only when he moved his arm upward. Before long, in hope of reward, the boy was raising his arm straight over his head.

The doctors were amazed, because they believed the boy could never learn to do anything. But Fuller's success did not convince others. It was quite easy to dismiss by saying that it would not work with persons of normal intelligence.

It was not until the 1960s that psychologists showed how effectively the behavior of intelligent people also could be shaped. They scored their successes behind the walls of an Illinois mental hospital.

As most psychologists admit, when people go into mental hospitals they sometimes become worse instead of better. They are shut away from their families and friends, and many come to believe that no one cares about them. Some spend days on end lying in their beds or slumped on a bench, staring at the floor. Some even refuse to eat.

Teodoro Ayllon decided to organize one of the hospital wards using principles that had been worked out in psychology laboratories. He had already been successful with individual patients.

For example, one woman was making life difficult for the hospital staff by hoarding towels. Whenever she saw a towel lying around, she'd snatch it up and carefully hide it away. She kept her own towels, the towels of other patients and any towels the nurses left unguarded.

It was plain that hoarding towels reinforced the woman in some way. Either she found pleasure in the presence of the towels themselves or else she enjoyed the attention she got from the nurses when they discovered her treasure trove.

The only way to stop the woman from stealing towels, Ayllon decided, was to arrange things so that towel-hoarding no longer reinforced her.

The nurses were told to stop scolding the woman and not to take her towels away. Instead, they brought more and more towels, until she was getting sixty towels every day. By this time the woman had a stack of more than six hundred towels. There were towels everywhere. Her dresser drawers were full of towels. The space under her bed was stacked with towels. Towels covered the top of her bed. Her closet was full ot towels.

Then, suddenly, the woman's behavior changed.

When a nurse arrived with a stack of towels, the patient said, "Don't give me no more towels." When a nurse walked through the ward, the woman said, "I can't sit all night long and fold towels." Finally, the woman begged, "Get these dirty towels out." The towels were removed and she never hoarded another.

A stack of towels no longer reinforced the woman. Instead, it made her uncomfortable. Towels had become as distasteful to her as a hot fudge sundae would become if you had just eaten a dozen without stopping.

Ayllon wondered if the principles of operant conditioning would make an entire ward run smoothly. Most patients were not towel hoarders, but if he could figure out a way to make active, helpful behavior reinforcing, the ward would be a pleasanter place for both patients and staff.

He solved the problem by inventing the token economy.

For thirty years, chimpanzees had been working for tokens. Chimps had learned to lift weights to earn plastic tokens, to save the tokens until they had the right number, and then to deposit them into a slot in exchange for grapes.

If chimpanzees would work for tokens, Ayllon saw no reason why mental patients would not. After all, outside the hospital they had worked in order to get the tokens we call money.

Ayllon and psychologist Nathan Azrin studied the patients. They learned that most of them enjoyed movies or TV, attending church, getting a chance to leave the ward, chatting with staff members and choosing the bed where they slept and the people with whom they ate. Not all patients liked all of these activities, but at least one thing on the list was reinforcing to nearly every patient.

Ayllon wanted to shape the patients' behavior so that they would do all the jobs that kept the ward running. If a ward was to be comfortable, it had to be kept clean and patients had to have food and clothes. There were floors to mop, laundry to sort, tables to set, meals to serve and disabled patients who needed help in keeping clean. Someone had to run the hospital store and the movie projector and go on errands.

Ayllon and Azrin decided that they would give patients tokens for working at these jobs and that the patients could exchange them for things they found reinforcing — movies, church, a chance to choose their own beds or to go to town to get chocolate bars and magazines at the store. Each job was worth a specified number of tokens, and each privilege cost the patient a certain number of tokens.

The patients were told about the plan and it began.

Most of the forty-four patients in the ward immediately began working at the various jobs and collecting tokens. They ranged in age from twenty-four to seventy-four, they were severely ill, and had been in the hospital for from one to thirty-seven years.

Only eight of the patients failed to change their habits in any way. These eight, whose lives seemed to be limited to eating and sleeping, wanted none of the rewards enough to work for them.

After the plan had kept the ward running smoothly for about three weeks, Ayllon changed the rules. He gave the patients tokens whether or not they worked. And they stopped working. The floor stayed dirty, the laundry piled up and sugar bowls and salt shakers sat empty.

When work brought no reinforcement, patients refused to do it. But when Ayllon again insisted that they work for their tokens, the patients went back to their jobs.

The experiment was a success. Ayllon had shown the power of reinforcement to change human behavior.

What is more, the patients had begun to act in

ways that would help them when they left the hospital. Because they were taking part in running the society of their ward, they would find it easier to fit into the society outside the hospital walls.

6

A Cottage in Kansas

Since Ayllon and Azrin invented the token economy, it has spread to many mental hospitals and to other places where psychologists are able to control the environment of their charges. But not everyone likes the idea. Some people say that the token economy takes advantage of helpless patients. It allows hospitals to make unpaid slaves out of people who cannot protect themselves.

Defenders of the token economy reply that it can turn helpless patients into useful citizens. In Parsons, Kansas, for example, psychologists showed that token economies can prepare some retarded children to live almost normal lives.

Mimosa Cottage in Parsons is home to retarded girls ranging in age from eight to twenty-one. These girls are so retarded that they cannot live at home or be taught in special classrooms in the regular school system. But steady reinforcement with tokens for jobs well done has enabled these girls to learn important skills and behavior.

When the girls first come to Mimosa Cottage, tokens have no meaning for them. They are merely metal discs stamped with the picture of a woman. You would recognize them as British halfpennies, but these girls can neither read nor write and know nothing of a country called England.

When a new girl completes a job properly — when she brushes her teeth or combs her hair or hangs up her clothes — she immediately gets a piece of candy. The sweet reinforces her behavior and makes it more likely that she will brush her teeth or hang up her clothes.

Gradually the staff members switch from candy to tokens.

At first the girl trades the token for candy as soon as she gets it. Then she must wait longer and longer to make her exchange. At last she learns to save several tokens to trade for something she wants very much, such as a toy from the cottage store, the right to play a record or a trip to the playground.

Now the girl is ready to live in a world in which

her behavior is slowly shaped toward the behavior of the world outside Mimosa Cottage. She learns to keep herself clean, to style her hair, to sew, iron and cook, to make change, to shop for groceries, to read simple stories and to dance.

When a girl refuses to do a specific task or if she misbehaves in some way, the punishment is quick, painless and effective. No one has to scold her and there are no spankings. She simply loses a number of her tokens.

Sometimes a girl with a special problem comes to Mimosa Cottage. She might throw tantrums or steal food from the trays of other children or — as one girl did — disrupt a meal by smearing butter over her face and clothes.

Attendants watch carefully for a time to see what usually happens before and after the girl misbehaves. Behavior modifiers believe that such behavior continues only because it is reinforced. Perhaps the girl had found that the only way to get attention from adults is by yelling or screaming or smearing butter on her dress.

Once they had decided what kind of reinforcement made the girl throw a tantrum or smear butter, the staff changed her environment so that her misbehavior was no longer reinforcing. They could pretend not to notice her screams or her dirty face. At the same time they found other acceptable ways for the girl to get the attention she so desperately sought.

Although some of the girls at Mimosa Cottage will

always have to live in an institution, others have gone back to the world outside.

Ellen is one of the girls who has graduated from Mimosa Cottage. At nineteen she works every day as a nurse's aide in the Parsons Nursing Home. There she helps care for elderly patients, doing all the little tasks that give them comfort. She makes beds, combs the patients' hair, sees that they have ice in their water jugs, adjusts their beds and pillows, feeds those who need help and pushes their wheelchairs outside where they can enjoy the sun. At night Ellen goes back to her foster home, where she helps her foster mother with the cooking and the housework and often baby-sits with her six-year-old foster brother.

Five years ago, when Ellen arrived at Mimosa Cottage, she couldn't tell the time, count money or even find her way to the dining room. Today she is a member of the community. Without the behavior shapers at Mimosa Cottage, she would still be living in an institution where attendants combed her hair, washed her face and guided her to the dining room.

7

Behind Bars

About the same time that Mimosa Cottage opened its doors, a different kind of token economy started in Washington, D.C.

Harold Cohen, who had seen the work of Ayllon and Azrin, set up an experimental program for delinquent boys. These boys were from fourteen to eighteen years old. They had two things in common. All were high school dropouts and all had been convicted of a crime — burglary, armed robbery, automobile theft, rape or murder.

Cohen's program, called CASE, was a part of the

federal prison system. In the world that Cohen and James Filipczak set up for these delinquent boys, each boy's behavior had immediate effects on his life.

In other words, the link between a boy's actions and the conditions under which he lived was as strong as the link between the pressure of the rat's paw on a bar and the drop of a food pellet into the cup.

Instead of using tokens, Cohen and Filipczak used points, which could be converted into money. Each point was worth one cent. This system used the same kinds of rewards the boys could expect to get in society once they had served their time — money and the things money can buy.

If these boys were ever to succeed in the world outside, they needed an education.

Therefore, they earned their points by going to school, by completing courses they chose to take and by scoring at least 90 percent on their tests. They could also earn bonus points by behaving in a courteous, responsible manner. They could lose points by fighting, stealing, cheating or using foul language.

From his weekly salary and bonuses, a boy could rent a private room, a private shower, buy his own clothes from a mail-order catalog and choose his own food at the CASE cafeteria.

Everything at CASE cost points, just as everything outside costs money. Washing a load of clothes cost points, enrolling in a class cost points, seeing a movie cost points, watching TV cost points, making a long-distance phone call cost points.

No boy at CASE had to work at his job of going to school. He could always go on relief. A boy on relief slept in a dormitory, wore regulation prison clothes, ate whatever was set in front of him and generally lived the life that most delinquent boys in a federal prison live.

There were other differences.

Working boys ate off china. Boys on relief ate from steel trays.

Working boys could use after-shave lotion, hair spray or any of the other toiletries they chose to buy. Boys on relief were restricted to soap and toothpaste.

Working boys could keep snacks in their rooms. Boys on relief could not.

Working boys could read all night and get up when they chose — as long as they got to class on time. Boys on relief had their lights turned out promptly at ten o'clock and were wakened at a set time.

Boys on relief knew they were in prison. Once two CASE boys who had plenty of points to pay for their expenses decided to go on relief. Within a couple of days they asked to return to the token system.

The relief dormitory stayed empty for most of the experiment.

The behavior of the boys at CASE was different from the behavior of boys in other parts of the federal prison system. CASE boys took care of CASE property. Nobody scrawled graffiti on the walls, carved his initials on desks, tore up books, smashed windows or furniture. The boys themselves even volunteered to plant grass and flowers and keep the playing fields in shape.

Half the boys at CASE were white; half were black. After a few minor clashes, blacks and whites settled down and lived together normally, without any racial problems.

Few of the boys had ever enjoyed their own rooms. At CASE they learned the pride of ownership. They built shelves, painted walls, used their points to buy rugs and kept their rooms clean.

As the experiment went on, striking changes appeared in the boys' attitudes toward life.

At first most boys spent their points for snacks, soft drinks, movies and other things that could be used up at once. After several months at CASE, they began to save their points and use them for clothing and other durable items and to buy gifts for their parents.

The boys learned to study and their tests showed it.

In addition to piling up credits that could be applied to later high school work, they showed changes in their IQ scores. The IQ of the average boy jumped about thirteen points during his year at CASE. Only one boy showed no gain in IQ, and one boy's score leaped twenty-seven points.

Such radical changes in the boys at CASE makes it plain that token economies are powerful shapers of behavior.

But the boys at CASE had to return to the outside world. No longer would they get immediate reinforcement for good behavior. Sometimes they would even be punished by their friends or by people they met for behavior that Cohen and Filipzcak had rewarded.

Most former prisoners wind up in jail again. After a year on their own, boys from CASE did much better than boys released from other federal institutions. The rate of CASE graduates who went back to crime was only one third of the rate among boys from other prisons.

Gradually, however, the outside world took over. Perhaps the boys began responding to old rewards in ways that had got them into trouble in the first place. At the end of three years in an uncontrolled environment, boys from CASE were doing almost as poorly as the average released prisoner.

Critics said that even if the CASE program did change' attitudes or behavior, the change was only temporary. A year of good behavior, they charged, could not justify the extra cost to the taxpayers of the token economy system.

Supporters of CASE point out that even though most of the boys eventually slipped back into their old ways the change in their behavior lasted for a full year after their reinforcers had been taken away.

They also maintain that a system like CASE prepares a person to live in a democratic society, while most prisons produce people who can live only in prisons. If a single year at CASE had such dramatic effects on boys whose lives showed a history of failure, then putting token economies in all our prisons might go a long way toward solving the problem of crime.

The three-year failure rate, supporters claim, is not the fault of CASE but the responsibility of society.

8

Not by Points Alone

At first behavior modification remained behind the walls of mental hospitals or prisons.

Even if operant conditioning did work in places where people were not free, so the argument went, reinforcement in the real world was a different thing altogether. No one could control the world of school children, factory workers or congressmen, and without strict control, a token economy would not work.

But back in Kansas, behavior shapers were taking the token economy into the community. Once again the subjects were delinquent boys, but these boys were not living in a federal institution.

Their home was a two-story house in a quiet family

neighborhood. The boys were from twelve to sixteen years old and all were three to four years behind in their schoolwork. Each of them had gotten into trouble with the law.

Judges sent the boys to Achievement Place, where six to eight delinquent boys live in a comfortable family home along with a pair of teaching parents.

Like CASE, Achievement Place uses points instead of tokens. The points may be spent for telephone, radio, record player or TV time, for between-meal snacks, for passes to go downtown or to visit home, for spending money and for bonds that may be exchanged for clothes or other desirable things.

The boys earn their points by keeping themselves well-groomed and their rooms clean, by helping around the house and yard, by behaving properly and by doing their schoolwork. When they break the rules, they are punished. They lose points.

Achievement Place is different from CASE in several important ways.

First, the boys help run their home, establishing the rules and deciding fair punishments at a nightly family conference with the teaching parents.

Second, the boys live in a family situation. Since Achievement Place opened, Elery and Elaine Phillips, the first teaching parents, have had two children of their own. Rules that work in a large boarding school, where students must live by strict schedules, don't fit the give and take of a family with a pair of toddlers.

Most important of all, the boys go to a regular school — often the same school they were attending when they were arrested — and each boy's teacher fills out a daily report card that describes his schoolwork and conduct. The checkmarks on the card determine the points he will win or lose for his day at school.

Boys who lived at Achievement Place did better in every way than either boys who were sent to a reform school or boys who were put on probation. Two years after they left Achievement Place, 90 percent of the boys were still in school and only 19 percent had had any trouble with the law. By contrast, only 9 percent of the reform school boys and 37 percent of the boys on probation were still in school, while over half these boys had been arrested.

But psychologist Dean Fixsen discovered that Achievement Place did not run on points alone. He was so pleased with the progress of the boys who lived with the Phillipses that he opened another home. To his surprise, the new token economy just didn't work.

When Fixsen watched the boys and the teaching parents at both homes, he soon discovered that points were not the only reinforcement handed out by the Phillipses.

They handed out praise as well.

When a boy did a job, they would compliment him. What is more, they gave careful instructions about each new job, and if they had to punish a boy by taking points away from him, they did it in a friendly manner, remembering to praise him if he was good-natured about losing his points.

The new Achievement Place was quite different. There the teaching parents were stern. They rarely praised the boys for a job well done. They never explained to them what they had done wrong.

For example, a boy would be ordered to clean a table. When he had finished, the teaching parent would look at the table and — instead of saying, "That's pretty good, but you missed a couple of spots on the far end" — would simply say, "That's not very good. You'd better do it again."

Fixsen found that the Phillipses had taught the boys in their care to accept criticism — the news that their work was not up to standard. They had also managed to use the boys' mistakes to teach them how to behave and cooperate with others.

Unlike the Phillipses, the teaching parents in the new home were more likely to make decisions themselves without letting the boys help.

It turned out that the relationship between the teaching parents and the boys was as important as the token economy to the success of Achievement Place.

But the techniques the Phillipses used with the boys at Achievement Place can be learned. Fixsen taught the couple whose token economy had failed just how the Phillipses treated their boys. Before long, they were doing just as well as the Phillipses.

Taxpayers might welcome Achievement Place because it is cheap to run. It costs less than half as much to care for boys who live there as it does to care for boys in a reform school.

Psychologists, however, are interested in Achievement Place because it showed that token economies can work without the complete control found in a mental hospital or a prison.

9

Bemod Goes to School

When Dean Fixsen set up Achievement Place, he had the advice and assistance of Montrose Wolf, a psychologist who already knew that operant conditioning worked with people. Several years before, Wolf had taught the teachers at the University of Washington nursery school to use behavior shaping with problem children.

For example, a three-year-old girl in the University nursery school didn't play with other children. She spent most of her time crawling around the schoolroom on all fours. Florence Harris, the director of the nursery school, told Wolf that the teachers had tried everything they could think of, but the child kept on crawling.

Wolf advised the teachers to do nothing for several days except to watch. They were to notice when the little girl crawled and when she stood up and walked.

The teachers watched and waited.

They discovered that the girl spent three hours and fifteen minutes out of every four hours on her hands and knees. She got up only when she had to — to go to the toilet, to wash her hands, to sit at the table and to get her coat from the coatrack.

The teachers also noticed something else. Whenever the little girl stood up, the teachers ignored her. But when she crawled, a teacher usually picked her up and cuddled her in order to make her stop.

Wolf told the teachers to reverse their behavior. When the child stood up, they should praise her. When she crawled around, they should look the other way and say nothing.

On the first day, the girl crawled into the bathroom, stood up at the basin and began to wash her hands. A teacher said, "Isn't it nice that you can wash your hands? And doesn't that warm water feel good?"

The little girl dried her hands, got down on all fours and crawled in to hear the storyhour. Later she stood up to get her coat, and a teacher said,

"What a big girl. You know where your coat is."

The next day the girl stood more and crawled less. At the end of four days, she was behaving like the other children. Wolf had taught the teachers to reinforce standing and to extinguish crawling.

It worked. When the little girl got no reward for crawling around like a baby, she stopped it.

After Wolf moved to the University of Kansas, he kept on shaping behavior. About the time that he was helping with Achievement Place, he began to take tokens into the schoolroom.

The place was a class for retarded children, and the tokens once again were points. Each time a child answered a workbook question correctly, he or she earned points. The points could be spent for candy, small toys, combs, ribbons or field trips.

The children's schoolwork improved at once; and the more points a subject was worth, the more correct answers the children gave.

Back at the University of Washington, psychologists were experimenting with the effect of punishment on schoolwork.

Each day an eleven-year-old girl was given four pages of arithmetic problems to solve. She was told that for every wrong answer on one of the pages, she would lose one minute of recess. The girl always knew which page of arithmetic carried the penalty; and she was told how many problems she missed, but never which problems. Nor did she get reinforcement. No one complimented her when she got all the problems right, and no one explained her mistakes.

As it turned out, the girl always managed to solve the problems on the page that affected her recess. But she did poorly on the pages where wrong answers carried no penalty.

If wrong answers on page two cost recess time, answers on page two would be correct. But if page-three errors cost recess time, page three would be done properly and the wrong answers on page two would climb sharply. When mistakes on any page cut into her recess time, she managed to solve the problems on all four sheets.

Punishment affected the girl's arithmetic just as it affected the behavior of rats and pigeons in the lab. As long as the punishment was given, the behavior changed. But as soon as the punishment stopped, behavior slipped back to the old ways.

Psychologists have discovered that punishment works best if it goes hand-in-hand with reinforcement. At Achievement Place the boys who got praise for taking the punishment of lost points gracefully did much better than the boys at the home where points were simply taken away.

In Illinois, teachers learned to use bemod in regular classrooms. One teacher was concerned about a first-grader whose mouth always looked red and raw.

David continually licked, rubbed and touched his

lips; he often complained that his mouth hurt. His teacher explained to David that she wanted to help him stop irritating his mouth. After that, whenever she saw that he was *not* touching his mouth, she praised him. She might say, "Your mouth is looking better, David," or "You are remembering very well." Sometimes she would simply smile, wink or hug him when his hands were not on his face. The teacher also told the class what a good job David was doing. She encouraged them to praise him as well.

Before she began the experiment, David had his hands at his mouth eight minutes out of every ten. Within a week he was touching his mouth only about two and a half minutes out of every hour. His mouth began to heal, and then it was time for Christmas vacation.

When David came back to school after the New Year, his mouth was normal. His parents may have reinforced him during the vacation, but it is likely that the pleasure of a normal, pain-free mouth was now by itself rewarding enough.

Other teachers have learned to help children do well in school by giving them praise and attention when they concentrate in class and finish their schoolwork. At the same time, these teachers ignore children if they stare out the window, daydream or fail to complete their work. They have discovered that scolding some students for dawdling, daydreaming or not finishing schoolwork makes them dawdle and daydream even more. In fact, sometimes scolding reinforces the very behavior it is intended to punish.

A student who believes he can't get attention for good work sometimes would rather have attention for bad work than get no attention at all.

Many people want to know if bringing bemod into the schoolroom helps most children learn.

Psychologists at the University of Kansas think it does. They have been working with poor children in all parts of the country. Their work, called Behavior Analysis, takes tokens and praise into Head Start classrooms and gets the children's parents to help.

In 1972, 7000 children were in a Behavior Analysis Head Start program. Don Bushell, Jr., reports that no matter where they have used the program, in the middle of New York City or on an Indian reservation in Arizona, the children enrolled do far better than children in other Head Start programs.

It works whether the children are white, black or Indian. It even works with children who do not speak English at home.

For a long time, psychologists have known that middle-class children do better in school than poor children. To the surprise of most psychologists, poor five-year-olds in the Behavior Analysis program make better scores than middle-class five-year-olds on reading, spelling and arithmetic tests.

But people who remember that after three years most CASE graduates did no better than boys who had gone to reform schools are sure to ask how children from these Head Start classes do in school. So far, so good.

Children who were in Behavior Analysis Head Start classes in 1968 were still doing better than other children as third-graders. Only time can show whether they will keep on doing better as eighth-graders or as high school students.

Behavior shaping in the classroom is not limited to tokens, praise and punishment from the teacher. Schoolbooks can also use reinforcement to help students learn. The principles behind teaching machines and programmed textbooks are the principles of operant conditioning.

Both books and machines work the same way.

The program starts by asking a question so simple that the student can answer correctly. At once the machine reinforces him by telling him he is right. With textbooks the student uncovers the answer and his reinforcement comes when the book's answer and his own answer are the same.

By small steps, the questions get harder and harder, but they all seem easy because the student is ready for them.

The student works at his own pace, taking his time if the program is difficult and working rapidly if it is easy. The machine will not move on to harder questions until the student answers the easier ones correctly. In the textbook, a wrong answer sends the student to a section devised for people who need extra help.

In some schools, machines teach six-year-olds to read. In universities, machines teach history or economics or psychology to college students.

Programmed textbooks are also widely used. Because the textbooks are cheap and easy to carry about, they have spread beyond the classroom, carrying operant learning into homes, businesses and even into prisons.

10

Into the Wilderness

As the successes of bemod grew and the news reached beyond the college classroom, businessmen began to pay attention. Some of them found it paid to listen.

Emery Air Freight, a company that ships goods all over the world, took positive reinforcement into every part of its operation. When Emery salesmen completed a programmed textbook course in how to present the company's services, sales jumped 28 percent in one year. When the employees who packed the freight for plane shipment used check sheets that told them at once how well they were doing, costs dropped $650,000 the first year. When the company began praising employees for jobs well done, workers were happier and the company made more money.

Vice President Edward Feeney estimated that positive reinforcement saved the company two million dollars in three years.

Bemod had finally entered the real world.

School is, after all, a place of rules and regulations, and many students are there only because the law says they must be. But employees can strike or even quit if they don't like their jobs or working conditions.

More and more businesses began to use the techniques that Emery Air Freight found were so profitable. Companies like Bell Telephone and General Motors discovered the power of positive reinforcement.

Behavior shaping kept spreading.

Psychologists in Utah showed that it would work even in the wide-open spaces. In Green Canyon, the litter of campers was spoiling the beauty of the wilderness. J. Grayson Osborne, Richard Powers and Emmett Anderson set about to change things. They chose a section of the canyon one-half mile long and one quarter of a mile wide to show that reinforcement could do what anti-litter signs and appeals to the conscience of campers failed to do.

First, they cleared the area of litter that had already been deposited. With the help of Boy Scouts, they collected 1676 pounds of cans, bottles, boxes, papers, automobile parts and garbage from that small square of wilderness.

Then they set up fifty-five-gallon oil drums as trash cans and placed a container of plastic litter bags nearby. They waited to see what people would do on their own.

They did very little. A few conscientious campers filled the bags and dropped them into the oil cans, but the litter began to accumulate again.

Now that it was known what people would do left to themselves, psychologists moved in with positive reinforcement. They attached large signs to the oil drums, telling campers that for every bag of litter deposited in the cans they could have either twenty-five cents or one chance to win twenty dollars in a weekly lottery. Above the litter bags there was a box that held registration cards for the campers to fill out.

Trash collection jumped.

Ten times as many bags of litter were put into the cans now that people were reinforced for their garbage collecting.

Most people were like the Las Vegas slot machine players. They chose the chance in the lottery instead of the twenty-five-cent reward.

For twenty dollars a week, a good-sized section of Green Canyon was kept clean.

The Utah psychologists pointed out that using lotteries to keep our parks and highways clean would work. And what's more, it was much cheaper than spending money on all the anti-litter billboards and TV ads — which don't work.

The laws in one state show that some people have stumbled onto the power of reinforcement, even if they call it something else.

In the state of Oregon, all bottles have deposits and throwaway bottles and cans have been outlawed. The litter on Oregon highways has dropped dramatically. The public is reinforced for keeping empty bottles out of the scenery.

And B. F. Skinner is smiling.

11

Change Yourself

Over and over again, most people do things they wish they would not do.

Some avoid schoolwork and one day discover they have failed algebra or English. Others eat too many french fries and pizzas and find themselves bulging in the wrong places. Still others drink too much alcohol or smoke too many cigarettes.

The failing student, the fat person, the alcoholic and the chain smoker all admit they lack self-control. If only they had will power, they say, they would study or give up fattening foods or stop drinking or smoking.

"But," they moan, "we're weak and can't resist temptation."

Behavior shapers say that talking about will power is silly.

"Behavior is maintained by its consequences," they repeat, which means that the rewards or punishments that follow each of our actions decide whether or not we will repeat them.

The punishments for not studying, over-eating, getting drunk or smoking are real, but they arrive so long after we skip homework or gorge on hot fudge sundaes or get drunk or smoke cigarettes that they have no effect. The reinforcements of free time; the cold, sweet taste of ice cream; the pleasant buzz from the third martini; and the taste, feel and smell of a cigarette are immediate. The rewards that follow our lack of self-control make it more likely that the next time we are tempted our control will be even weaker.

The way to develop self-control, say psychologists, is to decide which of our actions we want to change and to arrange our rewards and punishments so that we shape our own behavior just as psychologists shape the behavior of a delinquent.

Whether it's a short temper, a sweet tooth or a bad habit, our weaknesses can be overcome.

Suppose you are getting bad grades in three of your classes. You may think you are already getting plenty of punishment. Your teacher scolds you, your parents nag and you're on the verge of failing at least one class. It would seem that you should have changed your ways long, long ago.

But look at your situation more closely.

For a few days, notice exactly what you do. Whenever you have homework, you postpone it and instead watch TV, go to the movies or off with your friends. When you get to class, you spend most of the period hoping the teacher won't call on you. Because you haven't done your homework, you find it hard to follow the discussion. You begin to daydream and fall even farther behind.

The rewards of TV, movies and companionship come at once. The scolding comes later and — if you feel your parents ignore you — you may even find satisfaction in their nagging. Unpleasant attention is better than none.

Now suppose you rearrange your life so that your rewards change. You decide — and the decision must come from you — that in order to get good grades you must do your homework and pay attention in class.

You will have to keep strict records of your study time. Do this by making a graph like the one on the next page. Post the graph above your desk or on your bedroom door and each day record the number of minutes you spend studying.

For the first week, don't try to change your behavior. Study just as you normally do, thirty minutes or fifteen or five — or not at all. But be sure to mark the graph. At the end of the week you will have what

Study Time

Minutes Studied

3 hrs.
175
170
165
160
155
150
145
140
135
130
125
120
115
110
105
100
95
90
85
80
75
70
65
60
55
50
45
40
35
30
25
20
15
10
5
0

1 2 3 4 5 6 7 8 9 10 11 12 13 14 15 16 17 18 19 20 21 22 23 24 25 26 27 28 29 30 31

Date
October

psychologists call a *baseline*. That is, you will have a measure of the way you study now. This measure lets you see just how your behavior changes and how far you progress.

Now you are ready to begin. First, clear your study room of everything that might distract you. Do nothing except study when you sit down. No reading comic books or magazines, no writing letters, paring your fingernails. Reserve this place for studying.

Don't make your first goals too high. Give yourself one point for every five minutes of hard studying. Then trade your points for TV time.

Set up your own system of exchange. If your baseline was zero, make your TV time cheap. If your baseline was thirty minutes each day, make watching TV more expensive. A reasonable price might be six points for a hour of TV.

In class, keep track of what you are doing. Every five minutes write down whether you are looking out the window, daydreaming, doodling or listening to the teacher. You may find that just keeping track of the way you spend your time is enough to make you pay attention.

As the days pass you will find yourself studying for longer and longer periods. Gradually, you will begin to control your own behavior. Techniques like these have worked for many people.

Lisa, an eighth-grade girl, improved her history grade just by recording her behavior in class. She was worried about her schoolwork and had asked her counselor for help. The counselor consulted three psychologists who set up a program for her.

Lisa was given a sheet of paper and told to mark a plus on the paper when she was studying and a minus when she was not.

She agreed with her counselor that studying meant working on an assignment, facing the teacher, taking notes, facing another student who was answering the teacher's question, or reciting when the teacher called on her.

She marked the paper with a minus whenever she was out of her seat without permission, talking without permission, facing the window, handling things that had nothing to do with the assignment — such as a comb or purse — and doing homework for another class.

Before Lisa began to record her classroom behavior, an observer found that she spent only about 30 percent of her time studying. As soon as she started to keep her own observations, her study time zoomed to 80 percent of the period.

After Lisa had recorded for about two weeks the way she spent her classroom time, the counselor told her that the supply of recording slips had run out. Lisa's work plummeted. She spent only 27 percent of the period on study. The counselor gave Lisa more recording slips and at once her study time climbed back to 80 percent.

After a month had passed, the psychologists asked the teacher to begin praising Lisa for studying. She improved even more. Now Lisa was spending 88 percent of the period studying history.

The psychologists took away the recording papers. Lisa slipped slightly. Then the teacher was asked to stop the extra praise. There was another slight drop.

But the experiment had worked. Without keeping track of her behavior, without any extra praise from the teacher, Lisa was spending 70 percent of her history class studying history. Her grades were no longer a problem.

A student at the University of Chicago solved her school problems by learning to study at home. When she went to see psychologist Israel Goldiamond, she complained that she couldn't make herself study. Whenever she sat down and opened her books, she felt sleepy. As a result, her grades had begun to fall.

Goldiamond began by changing the position of her desk so that the girl no longer looked at her bed when she sat down to study. Then he told her to replace her dim forty-watt bulb with a strong light. The desk was reserved for study only. If she wanted to write a letter, read a comic book, eat a cooky or daydream, she was to get up and leave the room. The rule was study — and only study — when she sat at the desk.

At the end of the first week, the girl told Goldiamond she had spent only ten minutes at her desk. But she spent those ten minutes studying, which was what the psychologist wanted. Gradually, she was able to sit at her desk for longer and longer periods.

By the end of the semester she was studying three hours every day.

It would have been easy for this student to say, "I just can't study" and then fail her classes. Instead she found out what acts make up the process we call studying, and did them.

12

Shaping Your Shape

Some of us manage to study but have problems with food. We eat too much. Despite the fact that the extra pounds make us wince each time we look in a mirror or pull up the zipper on last year's clothes, we keep right on eating.

Overeating is a behavior that responds to the techniques of behavior modifiers. Psychologists who have studied fat people have noticed several things. Most of them have learned to associate eating with events that have nothing to do with real hunger. They eat when the clock says it's dinner time or when they see others eating or when they see or smell something that reminds them of food.

Fat people are also likely to eat faster than thin people. They often refill their forks or spoons the minute they place food in their mouths. They are likely to swallow their food without chewing it properly. A fat person may spend the same amount of time as a thin person at the dinner table, but the fat person will eat more food while the two are seated together.

If an overweight person wants to lose weight, the first thing he must do is to change his world so that he eats in response to different cues. No more reaching for peanuts or potato chips as soon as he opens a history book or turns on the TV. No more candy, bought when a display in a sweet shop window triggers a sudden urge.

Just as the student learns to study only at a desk, the overweight person must learn to eat only at the table. Food may be placed in the mouth only when the dieter is seated at the table, and the dieter may do nothing but eat while sitting there.

Sometimes this simple rule is enough.

Goldiamond persuaded one college student to follow these instructions. If he felt the urge to snack, he was to prepare his sandwich or open his bag of potato chips and then sit down at the table to eat it. Without reading or watching TV or studying.

It took only a week for the student to stop eating between meals. Switching on the TV was no longer a stimulus for a trip to the refrigerator. The student told Goldiamond that the rule had taken all the fun out of his forbidden snacks.

Besides establishing a single place to eat, the overweight person can also change the way he consumes food.

Instead of reloading his fork as soon as he places food in his mouth, the dieter can lay down the fork and not pick it up again until he has swallowed. He changes the stimulus for filling his fork from "food in the mouth" to "swallowing." He can also chew his food longer before he swallows it.

These two simple changes have important effects. First, they slow down the dieter so that he eats less food in a given period.

Second, they make less food more satisfying.

It takes about fifteen minutes after a person begins eating for his body to signal that his stomach no longer is empty. This means that when the dieter eats slowly he will be less likely to feel hungry when he gets up from the table.

Psychologists also teach dieters to keep account of the food they eat, just as Lisa kept account of her studying. Every mouthful from breakfast to the cooky picked up on a stroll through the kitchen to the casual candy mint and bedtime snack is written down and included in the day's calorie count.

Many overweight people are surprised to find that the tastes and bites and snacks between meals add up to as many calories as all their meals together.

Changing cues and watching behavior patterns often leads to eating less. But dieters can also control their behavior by setting up their own rewards.

Goldiamond had one of his overweight students buy a pair of trousers so small that he couldn't zip them up. Every few days the student was to put on the pants and pull up the zipper as far as it would go. Then he measured the closed track, using a ruler marked in millimeters. (A millimeter equals .039 inches!)

Because the millimeter is such a tiny measure, even a small weight loss allowed the student to close the zipper further, and each time the closed track measured another millimeter, the student was reinforced. He had visible proof that he was growing thinner.

Another reinforcement for dieters is concrete rewards — a new shirt, a record, a trip to the movies or money. Each time they lose a certain number of pounds or change their food or exercise habits, they give themselves the reward they've agreed upon.

The power of self-reward showed up among a group of overweight adults who worked with psychologist Michael Mahoney. Mahoney divided these adults, who all wanted to lose weight, into four groups.

One group had no instruction in self-control. Another group merely watched their own behavior and noted each time they ate. Members of the third group gave themselves money each time they lost a pound, while members of the fourth group gave themselves money when they regularly laid down their forks between bites or ate their meals in one place or walked several miles.

All the groups lost weight, but dieters who used rewards lost the most.

People who had no self-control instruction lost an average of three pounds during the eight-week experiment.

Those who recorded their food consumption lost eight pounds.

Those who rewarded themselves for losing weight lost fifteen pounds.

Those who rewarded themselves for changed habits lost twenty-one pounds.

At the end of the experiment, Mahoney taught the people in the group with no instructions to reward themselves for *both* weight loss and habit change. Now that they had mastered self-control techniques, they, too, lost weight rapidly. Self-rewards helped them shed another thirteen pounds over the next eight weeks.

Weight loss is never easy and the reward of a slim body is a long way down the road of self-control. But the person who pays close attention to his behavior and who supplements his picture of future attractiveness with some immediate rewards has a head start on the dieter who sticks to traditional methods.

13

Power to the People

Insomnia is another problem that can be handled by self-control.

When one man complained to psychologist R. R. Bootzin that he couldn't sleep a wink at night, the psychologist treated sleeping just as Goldiamond had treated Lisa's study problems. The sleepless man went to bed at midnight but could never go to sleep until three or four in the morning. He would toss in bed, worrying about his problems, then give up, switch on the late movie and finally fall asleep with the TV blazing away.

The man had spent so many sleepless hours in bed that the cues that make most people fall asleep — such as his own bed and a dark room — now meant restless hours of tossing and turning.

Bootzin advised the man to go to bed whenever he felt sleepy, but not to read or watch TV. If he couldn't sleep, he was to get up and go into another room. There he could read or watch TV until he felt sleepy. If he still could not fall asleep, he was to get up again and go back into the other room.

The first few nights, the man was in and out of bed several times. He had to go into another room four or five times each night. Then he found himself getting up less and less often, and by the time two weeks had passed, he was getting into bed and going to sleep almost at once.

Psychologists often teach people to substitute some other activity at a time when they usually do whatever they are trying to change. A dieter, for instance, might arrange to go for a ten-minute walk instead of sitting down to a cup of sweetened coffee and a jelly doughnut.

One woman who had been scratching herself for seventeen years switched to another habit and saw her rashes disappear.

Ever since she was four years old, this woman had had rashes on her body. She scratched herself almost continually, and at last came for help to psychologists D. L. Watson, R. G. Tharp and J. Krisberg.

In the beginning the woman merely kept a record

of her scratching. The first few days she scratched much less often, but after a week she was at her arms and legs as badly as ever.

The psychologists asked her to substitute a new response for her scratching. Instead of scratching whenever she itched, she was to stroke herself gently. Her scratching dropped off immediately, but she still found herself digging away at herself two or three times a day.

The following week she was told that unless she earned the proper number of points she would have to skip her daily bath. The only way she could earn points was by stroking instead of scratching. Now the scratching completely disappeared.

The final step was to substitute patting for stroking. It worked. The rashes cleared up, and in more than two years have come back only twice. Each time the stroking and patting has healed them quickly.

So if you should see a woman sitting on the subway and gently patting her arm, she might be practicing what psychologists call an *alternate response.*

The same Israel Goldiamond who helped University of Chicago students to eat less and study more found himself needing all the techniques of self-control he had developed. In 1970 Goldiamond was injured in an automobile accident. His spine was damaged. He was paralyzed.

Self-control could not repair a crushed spine, but it helped Goldiamond work his way back to a productive life.

Because Goldiamond knew that the results of a person's actions help shape his future behavior, he was able to analyze his own problems and shape his own life. He kept track of his movements, his emotions, his habits and his medication. Each time a problem came up, he noticed what events led to it.

Long before he was discharged from the hospital, he began going home on weekends, where he lay on a couch and taught his graduate psychology students.

Goldiamond will never walk. He must work from a wheelchair, but he still teaches at the University of Chicago. Self-control has enabled Goldiamond to help others with their problems. Some of those others are also handicapped. His months in the hospital and his own struggles have led him to adapt behavior modification techniques successfully to their problems.

As these successes show, self-control is within the reach of most people. A close look at the techniques psychologists use to help others develop self-control shows that behavior shapers are simply telling people to become aware of what they are doing and to discover why they are doing it.

Their message is that human beings are not helpless, but have the power to rearrange their worlds in more pleasant ways.

14

Is Punishment a Crime?

The movie *A Clockwork Orange,* which was filmed from the novel by Anthony Burgess, made many people uneasy about the discoveries of psychologists. It even sent some into a panic.

In that picture, Alex, who is serving a sentence for murder, volunteers for a new treatment that will allow him to be released from prison. He is given an injection, then strapped into a seat that resembles a barber's chair. Wires run from the cap-like headrest to a complicated machine. Clips hold up his eyelids so that he cannot close his eyes.

Alex is forced to watch a series of movies that portray beatings, rapes, torture and murder. The first picture delights Alex, who used to spend his evenings beating up helpless people just for kicks. "It was beautiful," he says.

But as he watches the films, he begins to feel sick and soon becomes acutely sick. His illness is the result of the injection, but — like Pavlov's dogs — he learns to connect the nausea, the pain and the pounding of his heart with the violence in the films.

After two weeks of this treatment, watching movies each morning and afternoon, Alex is released. He is no longer a danger to society. If he as much as thinks about hurting another person, he gets sick to his stomach.

But Alex, who lives in a violent society, can't protect himself. If he is attacked by others, he submits meekly to a beating, thinking, "It's better to be hit at like that than to be sick and feel that horrible pain."

Critics said that Alex had been turned into a moral robot, a man who could no longer choose between good and evil, a man who was forced to be good. Behavior shapers, said the critics, wanted to turn us all into a society of moral robots. We would all be clockwork oranges.

Strictly speaking, Alex's treatment had nothing to do with Skinner's operant conditioning. It was a throwback to the classical conditioning of Ivan Pavlov and the early behaviorism of J. B. Watson, because nothing Alex did affected his discomfort.

None of his responses — either by word or deed — could stop the pain or the picture. But it is the kind of vision that many critics of behavior shaping conjure up the minute they hear that psychologists are setting out to change someone's behavior.

When they heard about the programs in two California prisons, the critics said their predictions were coming true. They feared the day of the clockwork orange had arrived.

In these programs, convicts were strapped down and given a drug that paralyzed their bodies and made them feel as if they were suffocating. The men were terrified. They thought they were dying. During their panic, a prison doctor would lecture them on the evil of their ways, ordering them to change.

A doctor who worked at one of the hospitals said that two or three such treatments would "straighten out" a hardened criminal. But these treatments had no connection with either operant or classical conditioning. They were not operant-conditioning programs because nothing the prisoners did affected their discomfort. They were not classical-conditioning programs because there was no connection built up between any stimulus in the outside world and any response by a prisoner.

The programs no longer exist.

Public, press and government fury stopped the treatments shortly after newspapers printed the stories. But their memory lingers and shows what can happen when scientists forget they are working with human beings.

Psychologists call clockwork orange programs like the one that changed Alex an example of *aversive conditioning,* which means that the process is unpleasant. In a mild form, aversive conditioning is used by some behavior modifiers.

Suppose a man who drinks too much comes to a psychologist for help. The psychologist will probably use all the techniques of self-control described in the last chapters, but he might also use some form of aversive conditioning.

The man will be asked to imagine, over and over again, that he is opening a bottle of whisky, pouring some into a glass and drinking it. But he will also be asked to imagine that the sight, the smell and the taste of whisky make him sick. The psychologist will tell him to imagine the sensation of his upset stomach, the taste and smell of vomit welling up in his throat and mouth and pouring over his clothes.

No straps. No drugs. No trickery. No terror. The drinker's imagination can be enough to produce the same symptoms when he reaches for a drink that Alex in *A Clockwork Orange* felt when he thought about hitting someone.

The important difference is that the drinker knows exactly what he is doing and why. The drinker and the psychologist work together to condition the drinker so that alcohol will make him sick.

Some alcoholics have been helped by a kind of aversive conditioning that uses electric shocks.

Once more the drinker imagines opening the bottle of whisky, pouring some into a glass and drinking it. This time, just as he pretends he is lifting the glass to his lips, he signals the psychologist, who throws a switch. An electric current passes through a wire attached to the drinker's arm and he gets an unpleasant but not dangerous shock. This treatment is true punishment, because the shock comes *after* the patient has done something — if only in his imagination.

Both of these treatments will work with fat people, who can imagine getting sick over a piece of apple pie or get shocked as they dream about biting into a chocolate-covered caramel. The treatments will work with any other behavior a person dislikes.

But, because the person must use his imagination, they will work only when he *wants* to change.

Shock has been used in other ways. Some members of the bemod squad use it to stop a person from doing something that can harm him.

Once Malcolm Kushner was asked to help a high school student who had been sneezing for six months. The girl had been in the hospital with a kidney infection and, while she was there, the walls in the hall outside her room were painted. The smell of fresh paint started her sneezing and, no matter what the doctors did, she couldn't stop. Medicine was tried, trips to the country, treatments with a psychotherapist. None of them worked. Not even hypnosis stopped her sneezes, which came about once every forty seconds.

After a few treatments, in which Kushner shocked her each time she sneezed, the girl stopped. The sneezes never came back.

In another case, a six-year-old girl climbed everything that could possibly be climbed. No matter what her mother did, the girl climbed. Several times she fell and injured herself badly.

Psychologist Todd Risley first tried mild methods with the little girl. He tried to extinguish her climbing by ignoring it. She kept on climbing. He tried sending her to her room alone. She still climbed.

At last he used electric shock. Each time the girl climbed onto a chair or desk, she got a shock in her leg. She stopped climbing in Risley's lab, but kept on climbing at home. Under Risley's instructions, the mother began using shock at home. The climbing ended and so did the bruises and broken bones.

Electric shock, like spanking, is a painful form of punishment. But punishment does not have to hurt. When girls at Mimosa Cottage and boys at Achievement Place lost points for misbehaving, that loss was punishment.

If your parents deduct fifty cents from your allowance when you forget to carry out the trash, you have been punished. Chances are that next time you'll remember to put out the trash.

Any event that makes a person less likely to repeat his misbehavior is punishment.

Israel Goldiamond cured a stutterer with an unusual form of punishment. He put the stutterer in a booth and had him read aloud from a book. The student read at the rate of 140 words per minute. Each minute he also stuttered eleven times. Then, each time the student began to stutter, he heard his own recorded voice stuttering back at him. The sound of his own voice was so unpleasant that within eight days he was reading aloud at the rate of 256 words per minute — without a single stutter.

Another form of punishment is *time-out.*

The girl who lost a minute from her recess for every arithmetic problem she missed was punished by time-out. Some schools have set aside time-out rooms, barren rooms without books, pictures, records or radios, rooms where there is nothing to do. Whenever a student disobeys or disrupts the class, he is sent to spend fifteen minutes in the time-out room.

By itself, punishment doesn't always work the way psychologists would like it to.

The girl who was kept in from recess for missing arithmetic problems showed that she could solve the problems. But as soon as her mistakes no longer cost her recess time, she went right back to missing problems. Her schoolwork improved only as long as she was punished for her mistakes.

The same thing happened when Donald M. Baer tried to stop young boys from sucking their thumbs.

He showed them cartoons. Each time a thumb went into a mouth, the movies stopped. It worked beautifully. The boys stopped sucking their thumbs — but only as long as keeping their thumbs out of their mouths kept Woody Woodpecker cavorting on the screen.

Sometimes people react to punishment by running away. A child who was often beaten or spanked might simply run away to escape continual punishment. In one program meant to stop smoking, smokers were supposed to give themselves electric shocks each time they lit a cigarette. Half of them dropped out, saying that they didn't want to stop smoking badly enough to take the electric shock.

People also tend to avoid a person who punishes them.

This is the reason why many law-abiding citizens avoid the police. All their lives they have associated the police with punishment. A cop gives tickets and has the power to take lawbreakers to jail. The connection is so strong that people who have broken no laws feel uneasy when a policeman comes into view. As soon as he disappears, they are relieved.

Another problem with punishment is that it leads to more punishment. When electric shock or spanking or time-out works, people are likely to use it again. The person who does the punishing will be likely to use it the next time he faces a similar problem. His success has reinforced him for punishing others.

Is Punishment a Crime?

The person who gets punished is likely to punish others when he gets a chance. He has learned, from seeing punishment work on himself, that it's a handy way to change the behavior of others.

But the major problem with punishment is that it teaches us what *not* to do. We suffer for doing the wrong thing, but we're not always sure just what was the right thing — what it was we were supposed to do.

Some of the problems with punishment apply to negative reinforcement as well.

Negative reinforcement, in which changed behavior brings an end to pain or unpleasantness, is not often used by psychologists. Usually, negative reinforcement is combined with punishment. A child who is punished by time-out may be kept from the group for ten or fifteen minutes. If negative reinforcement is used, he stays away until his behavior changes in a specific way. If he is crying, he may be allowed to come back when he stops.

In one instance, punishment and negative reinforcement made a retarded adult work harder. Whenever he stopped working, the picture on his TV set blurred so that he could not watch it. The picture would not come into focus until he started working again.

Because of the unpleasant effects that may follow the use of punishment, some behavior modifiers prefer to stick to positive reinforcement. Others use painless punishment when rewards alone have no effect. Those who use painful methods resort to them only when a patient is doing something that threatens his own life.

Should a psychologist believe that punishment is necessary, he tries to find a way to reward some other behavior at the same time that he uses punishment.

If the psychologist rewards as well as punishes, he will be less likely to teach that punishment is a good method to use on other people. Nor will his patient be as likely to run away, rejecting the whole program because it's so unpleasant, as did the cigarette smokers who dropped out when they were required to shock themselves.

Is punishment a crime, then? Sometimes. If the person who is punished is not aware of what's going on. If he has not given his consent. If either the patient's life or health is threatened. If the punishment is excessive. If other, pleasanter methods would work just as well.

But when a behavior shaper talks about punishment, he is not talking about Alex, the clockwork orange.

15

Bringing Up Baby

The principles of operant conditioning began to shape the lives of human beings long before Ayllon started giving tokens to mental patients.

Back in 1944, about the same time that B. F. Skinner was teaching pigeons to guide missiles, a baby grew up in a box.

Deborah Skinner, Skinner's younger daughter, began life in the controlled climate of an aircrib. The crib, designed by Skinner to make life easier and pleasanter for both baby and mother, was a closed compartment about the size of a standard baby bed. The aircrib served as both bed and playpen.

One side of the baby box was made of safety glass, which could be raised and lowered. Inside the crib, the carefully regulated temperature and humidity kept the baby so comfortable that, day or night, she wore only a diaper.

When people heard about Skinner's invention, they were shocked. Only a cruel, unfeeling father would shut away his baby in a box. And if he wasn't cruel, he was at least unnatural.

Skinner answered by pointing out the advantages of the aircrib. Because the air was filtered, the baby needed a bath only once a week. What's more, she never had a cold or infection of any kind. Visitors with coughs and sneezes were no danger.

Because she wore no clothes, she could move about freely. She exercised more, and her muscles were much stronger than those of most babies. Her feet, which never knew booties, pajamas, socks or shoes, were almost as nimble as her hands, and she used her toes like fingers. No one worried about her smothering in her bedclothes. There were none.

Deborah came out of the crib to be fed, changed, bathed and played with. And because her mother had to spend less time soothing an unhappy baby, she enjoyed playing with her daughter.

If Deborah fussed, and was neither wet nor hungry, lowering the temperature by a degree or two changed her cries to coos. This discovery by the Skinners may mean that many fussing babies are simply too warm. Deborah never cried to get out of the aircrib, and she never objected when the Skinners put her back. She could always watch the family and play peekaboo through the clear window glass.

As Deborah passed her first birthday, she spent less time in the crib, but it served as her bed until she was nearly three.

More than thirty years later, only a handful of aircribs are in use, but the Skinner family is satisfied with them. Deborah's older sister reared her own baby in a box.

When someone brings Skinner to task for shutting his daughter away in an aircrib, he gently reminds them that she was no more shut away than the average baby — except from germs, drafts and summer heat. He points out that the barred sides of a normal crib and playpen are in truth a miniature jail, and then speculates as to whether spending one's first two years behind bars conditions a child for later life in a prison.

A child doesn't have to grow up inside an aircrib to feel the effects of operant conditioning. Behavior modifiers believe that, from his first hours on earth, every act of the smallest baby is either reinforced, punished or extinguished.

Some parents complain because their babies cry a lot when they are full, dry and apparently comfortable. Behavior shapers explain that spoiled babies are often babies whose parents pick them up each time they cry but leave them in their cribs the rest of the time.

The mother of such a baby might say to herself, "It would be fun to cuddle the baby now, but he's being good. I won't bother him."

Babies are reasonably bright animals.

A baby soon learns that when he cries, mother or father or Aunt Ellen picks him up. It's pleasant to be held gently next to a warm, human body. Babies enjoy cuddling as much as mothers do. And babies who are picked up each time they cry — and *only* then — are reinforced for crying. They become crybabies.

The mother of a crybaby can stop the wails if she is strong enough to listen to a lot of crying. The next time her baby cries — and he is neither hungry, wet nor in pain — she can leave him alone. If the baby cries long enough without the reinforcement of cuddling, his crying will undergo extinction. But if the mother forgets the rules of operant conditioning, she will find herself in trouble.

Suppose her baby cries until he gives up two or three times in a row. Then, the next time he cries, Aunt Ellen is visiting. She rushes in and picks up the poor, little baby. Her cuddling puts him on a schedule of intermittent reinforcement. The baby is on the same schedule as Las Vegas gamblers. He has learned that crying sometimes pays off.

Behavior shapers have even offered to help mothers with the sometimes distressing chore of toilet training. Although many children, about the time they are two years old, move from diapers to pants as if by magic, others remain in diapers for months or even years.

Mothers whose children are late in learning to use a toilet often become impatient and resort to punishment. But a two-year-old who is spanked when he comes to his mother with a wet diaper thinks that he's being punished for coming to his mother — not for losing control.

Nathan Azrin, who helped Ayllon invent the token economy, and Richard Foxx say that any mother who is willing to spend four uninterrupted hours with her child can toilet train him.

Their method is pure behavior shaping. The child gets lots of good things to drink and salty snacks to eat, a precaution that makes sure he needs to use the toilet often. Then, each time he uses his potty chair, he gets praised to the skies. Between his trips to the toilet, as he munches his potato chips and drinks his lemonade, he practices toilet training a doll. He takes down its pants, sets it on the potty chair and tells it what a good child it is for using the toilet.

Azrin and Foxx go far beyond training a child to tell his mother when he must use the toilet. Their method produces a child who takes full responsibility, even emptying his potty chair after each use, flushing the toilet and washing his hands.

These behavior modifiers also have a method for training bed wetters. Their method takes only one night and saves older children from having to take a drug that often has such unpleasant side effects as loss of appetite or an uncomfortable rash.

The power of behavior shaping does not stop with crying babies and wet diapers. Every act of the growing child — eating, talking, playing, sleeping — is affected in some way by the responses of those around him.

16

Baby See, Baby Do

As psychologists began to use behavior modification with people, they discovered that work with animals had not told them everything about operant conditioning. Human beings often changed their behavior without reward or punishment. All that was necessary was for them to see someone else rewarded or punished. They seemed to apply the results of other people's experiences to themselves.

Psychologists call this method of shaping behavior *modeling*, and many members of the bemod squad use it.

The person who actually has the experience acts as a model for those watching him. The most powerful models for young children are their parents. As children grow, visitors often say, "Dennis is a chip off the old block."

Behavior modifiers would say that Dennis has modeled his actions on those of his father. If Dennis and his father both have quick tempers, it's probably because Dennis has seen his father reinforced for losing his temper.

If Daddy throws down the paper and shouts at Mother, it works. He gets his way. On the other hand, if Daddy rarely raises his voice and becomes quiet and withdrawn when things annoy him, Dennis is likely to behave in the same way.

When psychologist Albert Bandura studied a group of children, he found that boys who fought a lot had parents who lost their tempers easily. Boys who never fought had parents who controlled their tempers. But the differences were not due to modeling alone. The parents of non-fighters discouraged fighting, but did not punish their sons if they got into a fight.

The parents of boys who fought a lot acted differently. They punished their sons if they struck their mothers or fathers but didn't interfere if the boys fought with their brothers and sisters. Furthermore, if the boys got into fights with other children, their parents praised them.

By itself, modeling is a powerful tool in helping a

child to overcome his fear of dogs, cats, mice, snakes or the dark.

Bandura and F. L. Menlove studied a group of young children who were afraid of dogs. These boys and girls would not play with dogs, refused to pet them and became frightened if a dog came near.

Bandura and Menlove divided the children into three groups. Each group of children saw a movie. One group watched a child walk up to a dog that was inside a playpen, kneel down and pet it, romp and play games, and finally lie down on the grass with his arms around the animal and his face close to its open mouth.

The second group of children saw the same kind of movie. Instead of a single child playing with a single dog, they watched several children of various ages playing with dogs that ranged from tiny Chihuahuas to massive Great Danes.

The third group of children watched a movie that had no dogs in it at all. By including them in the experiments, Bandura and Menlove could be certain that the child models in the film were responsible for any changes in the behavior of the other children.

After the movies were over, Bandura and Menlove gave each child a chance to play with a dog.

The children who had watched films of children playing with dogs seemed to have lost much of their fear. Most were now willing to pet and play with a dog. The children who saw the movies without dogs were as afraid as ever. But when the psychologists showed them the film of several children playing with dogs, their fears also disappeared.

A month later, Bandura and Menlove saw all these children again. Their fears had not returned, but the boys and girls who saw several models play with different kinds of dogs were braver and played more freely than the children who had watched only one child play with one dog.

Modeling goes on all the time. Sometimes when parents think they are teaching their children one thing, the children are learning just the opposite.

Suppose a parent spanks his son for fighting with the boy next door. The punishment stops the fighting, but his son has learned that hurting other people is a good idea. He has just seen it work. His father punished him and he stopped fighting.

Or suppose that parents tell their children that they must always be truthful. The parents say that it is wrong to lie.

The children then hear Mother refuse an invitation to play cards with the Joneses, saying that Father has to go to a meeting. Mother puts down the phone, turns to Father, and says, "I told Mrs. Jones you had a club meeting. She's such a bore I just couldn't face another evening with them."

The next week the children hear Father brag about how he has cheated on his income tax and saved himself eight hundred dollars.

Studies have shown that when models say one thing but do another, children who watch them tend to copy what they do. Actions do speak louder than words. The children in the family just described may learn to say that lying is bad, but they are likely to lie themselves. Their parents have literally taught them to lie.

Children find other models, too. Their brothers and sisters, friends, teachers, neighbors and even the actors they see on TV. A number of studies have shown that after children watch violent cartoons their play is likely to be full of aggressive talk and action. A child who has just seen the coyote and the road-runner try to destroy each other is likely to hit if he is given a chance.

When adults laugh at the toddler who teeters around in her mother's shoes, they should remember that children learn more from models than how to dress.

17

Parents Join the Squad

Not all behavior shaping in the home goes on without the parents' knowledge. For instance, Vance Hall, with the help of other psychologists, taught a mother to shape her daughter's behavior.

The girl, who was ten, neglected her work. She either practiced her clarinet for just a few minutes or didn't touch it at all. She forgot to work on her Campfire Girls project, and she never finished the books for her school book reports.

Hall advised the mother to work on only one behavior at a time. They decided to use punishment.

Clarinet practice came first. The girl was told she would have to practice for thirty minutes each day. If she practiced any less, she would have to go to bed one minute earlier for each minute of practicing she skipped. Her practicing for the day zoomed from ten minutes to thirty.

But she was still neglecting her other activities.

Four days later, the mother informed her daughter that she must also work thirty minutes each day on her Campfire projects. Same conditions. To bed a minute earlier for each required minute not spent on her project. Again there was an overnight change. Now the girl was both practicing her clarinet and working on her project.

Four days later, the mother added reading to the list.

The girl now had to read for half an hour each day or go to bed early. Again the success came overnight. In just over two weeks, the girl was spending half an hour a day on each of her three assignments.

Some parents, instructed by University of Kansas psychologists, use token systems successfully in their homes.

Children earn points when they make their beds, hang up their clothes, empty the trash and feed the dog or cat. They lose points when they forget these chores. They can win extra points by vacuuming the carpet or cleaning the bathroom and lose points by teasing each other, fighting, bickering or whining. After earning a certain number of points that take care of basic privileges, the children can spend their points on outings like family picnics or movies.

The difference between paying or withholding an allowance and the point system lies in its exactness. Each task is defined.

For example, a bed is made when the sheets and blankets are tucked in, there are no large wrinkles and the pillow is properly under the spread.

Violations are also defined. Bickering is a verbal argument conducted in a loud voice.

Precision means that the system is not likely to break down with disagreements over when one earns or loses privileges. No one has to decide whether making a bed by simply pulling up the spread qualifies for an allowance or whether David and Susan are bickering or merely having a discussion.

Occasionally, parents object to points or other concrete rewards for good behavior on the grounds that people should behave properly without payment.

Psychologist Roger McIntire, illustrating the point, tells about one father who voiced this opinion. Then, when he was thanked for coming in to help with his son's problems, he replied, "That's all right. We're out on strike for a raise."

The fact that he refused to do his own job without more payment had escaped his notice.

It's not always necessary to resort to points or money to change the behavior of children. Attention, praise and encouragement often shape behavior as effectively as concrete rewards do. Parents can treat behavior problems just as the attendants at Mimosa Cottage handled the girl who liked to smear butter over her clothes.

Suppose a girl continually fights with her brother.

The first, and the hardest, thing the parents must do is to stop reinforcing the girl's fighting. When she starts a quarrel, they must not punish her, scold her or even notice that one is going on.

Next, they should reinforce her whenever she does something that cannot be done while she's fighting. If she sits quietly in a chair and reads a book or plays a friendly game of Monopoly with her brother, or watches TV without arguing, her parents must praise her. Gradually, the fighting will disappear and her friendly behavior will increase.

For the problems of babies, toddlers, school children and teenagers, behavior modifiers have come up with answers based on the principles of conditioning. They offer to help eliminate fears and fighting and to shape helpful behavior.

They believe that their successes show how we can make houses into happy homes.

18

Back to the Battle

Agroup of clean, well-fed babies are crawling about on the floor of a clean but uninteresting room.

Bowls of beautiful roses and gay picture books line the floor behind them. The bright blossoms and the colorful books are spots of beauty against the bare walls. Nurses turn the infants so that they can see the display. The babies gurgle with delight and crawl toward the inviting objects.

As their tiny fingers reach out to touch the petals or grasp the pages, sirens suddenly shriek, bells clang and electric currents course through the floor.

Naturally, the babies scream with fright and pain.

Before long, in the days ahead, they whimper and turn their heads away at the mere sight of a flower or a book.

These babies appear in Aldous Huxley's *Brave New World,* a story about a future in which children are conditioned by birth to be happy in the lives chosen for them by the state. Children who are destined to become Deltas, workers near the bottom of society, are conditioned to dislike beauty, nature and books.

As these children grow, they hear a voice each night in their dreams. Over and over the recorded voice says, "I would not want to be an Alpha. Alpha children wear gray. They work much harder than we do. I'm awfully glad that I'm a Delta, because I don't work so hard."

When Delta children become adult workers, they will have plenty to eat, warm clothes to wear, comfortable beds and all the manufactured objects they can use.

But they will have no desire for any of the privileges enjoyed by the ruling Alphas. They have been taught to hate books, because books carry dangerous ideas. To hate nature, because looking at mountains and trees and lakes consumes nothing made at a factory. They are taught this because the economy of the brave new world wholly depends upon full production and consumption.

But still these Delta children will be happy. Because all Deltas are conditioned as babies to dislike and fear ideas, they will never, never disturb society. They will be content to plod along, day after day, doing all the dull jobs that keep factories humming.

Although Huxley wrote *Brave New World* many years before Anthony Burgess thought of the clockwork orange, both writers warned us against a society that uses scientific knowledge of human nature to control human behavior.

Many people who object to the work of behavior modifiers believe that bemod will lead us straight into a nightmare world of dictators. But dictators existed long before Skinner told the world about his pecking pigeons and his rats that pressed bars. Tyranny flourished for centuries without any scientific knowledge of human behavior.

Behavior modification is neither democratic nor totalitarian. It takes no sides.

It is a method, a way of shaping human behavior, that came from millions of hours of patient observation and experimentation with both animals and people. The method has made many human lives happier. But behavior modifiers would be the first to agree that their methods can also be used for evil purposes.

They have, they insist, only explained to us the way human behavior has always been shaped. Just as a knife can be used by a housewife to slice bread, by a surgeon to remove an appendix or by a murderer to slit a throat, so bemod can be used both to help people and to oppress them.

Behavior shapers themselves believe that if their principles are adopted in prisons, hospitals, schools, businesses and the home, crime will decrease, children will learn more, employees will be happier, businesses will make more money and life will be more pleasant.

Used properly, bemod can do some of these things all of the time and all of these things some of the time. The big problem is to see that it is used properly.

If the bemod squad had remembered Skinner's words and refused to use aversive conditioning, there would be much less criticism and fewer abuses.

But many psychologists lack the patience to rely upon positive reinforcement. Punishment is quick. Painful punishment is even quicker, and, when used with reinforcement, enables psychologists to solve behavior problems in a few short sessions — problems that respond to positive reinforcement alone only after weeks or months or years of patient effort.

The fact that clockwork orange programs could turn up in places where people cannot protect themselves makes many critics uneasy about all the practices of behavior modification. They are uneasy because they know from studying the writings of the behavior shapers that each time punishment is successful it is more likely to be used again.

Yet Skinner has been careful to warn that under

certain conditions people who control the behavior of others will themselves become cruel. When two people are together, each normally affects the other's behavior. This is true, says Skinner, even when one of the pair is a tiny baby and the other a strong adult.

If it seems odd to think of a baby as a behavior shaper, consider the way its cries, coos and smiles shape a mother's behavior.

The baby cries until he is taken up. Negative reinforcement. The next time his mother hears him cry, she rushes to pick him up.

The baby smiles and coos when his mother plays with him. Positive reinforcement. She is likely to play with him again.

The baby cries the minute his mother puts him back into his crib. Punishment. His mother promptly takes him up.

Skinner would say that, while the mother controls her baby, the baby countercontrols his mother.

Once we move into the world of institutions, however, countercontrol drops off.

Patients in mental hospitals, convicts in prisons, children in orphanages and old people in homes for the aged lose the power to control their controllers. Guns, bars, walls or physical weakness make objections useless. No one can escape, punishment follows protest and none of the officials who run these institutions cares if inmates cry, curse or complain.

It was just this lack of countercontrol that made

mental hospitals the ideal place for psychologists to work out programs like token economies.

But when controllers are free from countercontrol, they tend to become callous and cruel. For these reasons, strict rules should surround any use of bemod in institutions — as strict rules should protect inmates no matter what programs are used.

Outside institutions, countercontrol always affects conditioning.

At present, most countercontrol is haphazard, and those who use it often are not aware of what they are doing. But as knowledge of bemod spreads, people generally considered the captives of their controllers will learn to use the techniques deliberately. School children in a small California town, for example, learned to use behavior modification on their parents and teachers. The result was a pleasanter life for everyone.

Psychologists Paul Graubard and Harry Rosenberg started their work with children in special classes who were considered behavior problems. Because they had been labeled as troublemakers, teachers tended to treat them in ways that reinforced their bad behavior. Teachers expected the troublemakers to break rules, so they did. Teachers rarely praised them when they followed the rules, so they didn't. Generally, the teachers reinforced the students for misbehaving.

Graubard and Rosenberg taught these students to reward their teachers each time the teachers acted in a pleasant and helpful manner. If a teacher was friendly, the student would say, "I like to work in a room where the teacher is nice to the kids."

The students learned to smile, look the teacher in the eye and sit up straight when the teachers were helpful. They thanked the teachers for explaining problems and rules.

The troublemakers also learned to treat unpleasantness by ignoring it. When a teacher made a hostile remark, the student would pretend not to hear it. If a teacher persisted in his unpleasantness, the student would use mild punishment, saying, "It's hard for me to do good work when you're cross with me."

Within a few weeks, the atmosphere in the school was different. Teachers said the students had changed. They were no longer insolent troublemakers who broke every rule they could find. Students said the teachers had changed. They were no longer grouchy and unfriendly, just waiting for a chance to get a student in trouble.

Both were right. Everyone had changed.

As the students shaped the behavior of the teachers, the pleasant and helpful responses of the teachers reinforced the suddenly courteous behavior of the former troublemakers.

Control and countercontrol combined to solve many of the school's problems.

As the students realized the power of behavior shaping, they became self-confident and lost interest in making the teachers feel uncomfortable or in disrupting the class.

When the students saw how well bemod worked at school, some of them began to use it at home. For example, the mother of one girl never had meals ready on time and often let the laundry pile up until members of the family had no clean clothes to wear. The girl began to shape her mother's behavior as she had shaped her teacher's behavior.

It worked. The mother became efficient at her household chores and even gained self-respect as she found that she was a more capable person than she had believed.

Our first impulse on hearing of the successful student behavior modifiers is to laugh and say, "Just wait until those parents and teachers find out what was going on. They'll be outraged and that town will go back to its old, unpleasant ways."

We would be wrong.

When they learned about the project, teachers were enthusiastic and parents were pleased. None found fault with the young behavior shapers. Parents had become aware of their children's specific needs. One father said that for the first time his son began to talk to him about things he could do to be of help.

Despite successes like these, some critics continue to object to the deliberate use of conditioning — even praise — on the grounds that any attempt to shape the behavior of others is wrong.

They make this objection in speeches and articles meant to shape the behavior of others into opposing behavior modification. Their position seems to be that as long as people don't know precisely what they are doing and exactly how it affects the behavior of others it's all right to do it.

The same critics also forget that our schools are *designed* to change behavior. Public education is supposed to turn out moral, democratic citizens. The only way it can do this is to condition children, making murder, robbery and other crimes unthinkable and the idea of a dictatorship repellent.

Other opponents of bemod complain that positive reinforcement is all right, but that it just won't work. When people realize that the praise they get is meant to shape their behavior, the behavior will go unshaped.

The work of the bemod squad shows that this charge is wholly inaccurate. As long as the praise is sincere, it will continue to change behavior. A compliment given for an unappreciated act rings hollow, but because reinforcement comes for acts the behavior modifier wants, the praise is generally sincere.

It works.

The bemod squad has one quality that makes behavior modification less dangerous than some other means we use to persuade people. Its members are frank about their aims, saying that they plan to change behavior and often just how they propose to do it. As long as behavior shapers remain in the open, they are the safest kind of manipulators to have around.

The battle over bemod really boils down to three related questions:

Who is going to control the behavior?

Why is it being controlled?

Does the control limit a person's freedom?

Behavior modification in a dictatorship is dangerous. There's no argument on this point.

In a democratic society, however, the controllers are teachers, parents, therapists and employers. Students, children, patients and workers remain free to countercontrol, as the California students have proven.

And self-control poses no danger to society at all.

One of this country's founding fathers was skilled in its techniques. Benjamin Franklin decided that thirteen different virtues, from temperance (neither eating nor drinking too much) to humility (imitating the conduct of Jesus and Socrates), made up the perfect man.

Franklin kept a little book filled with charts on which he marked each time his behavior violated one of the virtues. Each week he concentrated on a different virtue. Franklin found that when he recorded his lapses from grace the number of his faults decreased sharply.

If behavior is controlled to keep a political party in power or to send a nation to an unnecessary war, it is clearly wrong.

But most behavior shapers work to help people get rid of unwanted habits or to learn to act in desired ways. They teach them how to study, how to stop eating or drinking too much, how to overcome fears. They show them that by overcoming bad habits and unwanted behavior, the individual is able to act in ways that were closed to him before. Those who no longer feel compelled to smoke cigarettes or nibble candy all day feel more — not less — free.

Some philosophers are uncomfortable because they see behavior modification leading to a world of moral robots. They want man free to choose between good and evil. Neither Alex nor the Deltas had that choice.

No one wants a world shaped by aversive conditioning — not even the bemod squad.

Praise and reward, combined with mild, pain-free punishment, is not likely to lead to the abuses that philosophers fear. Used properly, bemod could help us to reach a world in which individuals wished and worked to be responsible and sensitive citizens.

Perhaps the answer to the problem posed by behavior modification is not suppression but education. Knowledge is power. The more people know about the promises and possible abuses of behavior shaping, the less any of us have to worry about the world of the clockwork orange.

GLOSSARY

AIRCRIB: a closed compartment, about the size of a standard
baby bed, that serves as both crib and playpen. The aircrib
was invented by B. F. Skinner.

ALTERNATE RESPONSE: a response that is substituted for a person's customary response to a stimulus.

AVERSIVE CONDITIONING: any conditioning that uses an unpleasant stimulus to change behavior. When behavior modifiers employ aversive conditioning, they may use either negative reinforcement or punishment.

BEHAVIORISM: the school of psychology that limits its study to
the behavior of man and animals. Behaviorists do not study
"mind" or "consciousness" or "feelings"; they are interested
only in behavior they can observe and measure.

BEHAVIOR MODIFICATION: changing behavior by controlling the
results, or consequences, of the behavior. Also called behavior shaping.

BEHAVIOR SHAPING: see behavior modification

GLOSSARY

CLASSICAL CONDITIONING: a simple form of learning. A neutral stimulus (such as a bell) comes to stand for a potent stimulus (such as food) and brings forth the response that the person or animal usually gives to the potent stimulus.

CONDITIONED RESPONSE: the response (such as drooling) that, after conditioning, follows a stimulus (such as a bell) which once brought forth no such reaction.

CONDITIONED STIMULUS: the stimulus (such as a bell) that, after conditioning, brings forth the response (such as drooling) that originally followed the unconditioned stimulus (such as food).

CONDITIONING: a change in a person or animal's behavior as a result of the influence of the environment. In classical conditioning, the change comes about when a formerly neutral stimulus becomes connected with an unconditioned stimulus. In operant conditioning, the behavior changes as the animal or person interacts with the environment.

CONTINUOUS REINFORCEMENT: a schedule of reinforcement in which each response of an animal or person is followed by a reinforcer.

ENVIRONMENT: the surroundings of any plant, person or animal. These conditions affect both the organism's present state and its growth and development.

ESCAPE TRAINING: a form of aversive conditioning in which an animal can end an unpleasant stimulus by responding in a certain way. Escape training uses the process of negative reinforcement.

EXTINCTION: the disappearance of a behavior because the person or animal no longer is reinforced for producing it.

INSTINCT: an unlearned behavior that a person or animal performs correctly the first time the appropriate circumstances arise. Practice will improve the performance of many instinctive behaviors, such as flying.

INSTRUMENTAL CONDITIONING: see operant conditioning

INTERMITTENT REINFORCEMENT: reinforcing a person or animal for a particular behavior for only part of the time; also called partial reinforcement.

MODEL: a person who demonstrates a behavior and whose actions are imitated by those watching the demonstration.

MODELING: The process of shaping behavior by demonstrating a response or a series of responses, which a person imitates.

NEGATIVE REINFORCEMENT: any stimulus (such as electric shock) whose removal makes it more likely that the animal or person will repeat his behavior.

OPERANT CONDITIONING: a form of learning in which an animal or person's actions are either reinforced or punished; also called instrumental conditioning or Skinnerian conditioning.

PAVLOVIAN CONDITIONING: see classical conditioning

POSITIVE REINFORCEMENT: any stimulus (such as food) whose presentation makes it more likely that the animal or person will repeat his behavior.

PRIMARY REINFORCER: anything, such as food or water, that without any training strengthens a behavior.

PUNISHMENT: a penalty that follows behavior and makes it less likely that a person or animal will repeat the behavior.

REINFORCER: something that makes it more likely that an animal or person will repeat the action that came before the reinforcer.

RESPONDENT CONDITIONING: see classical conditioning

SECONDARY REINFORCER: something that, because it has become associated with a primary reinforcer, strengthens a behavior.

SELF-CONTROL: a form of behavior modification in which the person shapes his own behavior by arranging his own reinforcements.

SKINNERIAN CONDITIONING: see operant conditioning

STIMULUS: some event or object that causes a person or animal to react; the stimulus may be in the outside environment or within the person or animal.

TIME-OUT: putting a person in a neutral place, away from people and objects that might reinforce him. The isolation is painless punishment; if the person's behavior must change before he leaves the neutral place, it also acts as negative reinforcement.

TOKEN: a metal or plastic disc that acts as a secondary reinforcer. It may be exchanged for food, toys, money or privileges.

TOKEN ECONOMY: a system in which tokens are used as secondary reinforcers; later, the tokens are exchanged for primary reinforcers.

UNCONDITIONED STIMULUS: the original, potent stimulus (such as food) that brings forth a response (such as drooling) in classical conditioning.

INDEX

INDEX

INDEX

INDEX